A RETREAT WITH OSCAR ROMERO AND DOROTHY DAY

Other titles in the A Retreat With... *Series:*

A Retreat With Oscar Romero and Dorothy Day

Walking With the Poor

Marie Adele Dennis

ST. ANTHONY MESSENGER PRESS

Cincinnati, Ohio

Scripture citations are taken from the *New Revised Standard Version Bible*, copyright ©1989 by the Division of Christian Education of the National Council of Churches of Christ in the U.S.A. and used by permission.

The excerpts from *The Word Remains: A Life of Oscar Romero*, by James R. Brockman, S.J., copyright ©1982, by Orbis Books, are reprinted with permission of the publisher.

The excerpts from *Love Is the Measure: A Biography of Dorothy Day*, by Jim Forest, copyright ©1986, 1994 by James H. Forest, are reprinted with permission of the publisher.

The excerpts from *Meditations, Dorothy Day*, edited by Stanley Vishnewski, copyright ©1970 by The Missionary Society of St. Paul the Apostle in the State of New York, is reprinted with permission of Paulist Press.

The excerpts from *Voice of the Voiceless: The Four Pastoral Letters and Other Statements*, translated from the Spanish by Michael J. Walsh, copyright ©1985 by Orbis Books, are reprinted with permission of the publisher.

The excerpts from *Dorothy Day, Selected Writings: By Little and By Little*, edited and with an introduction by Robert Ellsberg, copyright ©1992 by Orbis Books, are reprinted by permission of the publisher.

The translations from *Piezas Para Un Retrato*, by Maria Lopez Vigil, copyright ©1993, by the Universidad Centroamericana Jose Simeon Canas, are reprinted with the permission of the translator, Eugene Palumbo.

The excerpt from "Remembering a Bishop," by Tom Quigley, is reprinted with permission of *The Witness*.

Cover illustrations by Steve Erspamer, S.M.
Cover and book design by Mary Alfieri
Electronic format and pagination by Sandy L. Digman

ISBN 0-86716-261-9

Published by St. Anthony Messenger Press
Printed in the U.S.A.

Contents

Preface

It is hard to imagine a task more inspiring than that of writing about these two great figures of the twentieth century. Word of Oscar Romero's assassination in March 1980, followed so closely by my friend Yvonne Dilling's chilling account of the massacre by their own military of hundreds of Salvadoran *campesinos* (Latin American farm laborers) as they tried to cross the Rio Lempa to safety in Honduras (May 1980), irrevocably captured my attention and concern about the repression in El Salvador. At the Center for New Creation, where I was working at the time, we were already fully engaged in the work of solidarity when the four United States churchwomen were murdered in December 1980. We learned of their disappearance and death at a board meeting of Network, the Catholic social justice lobby. Many women on the board at that time were personal friends of the murdered missionaries; the impact was immediate and tremendous.

Since that time, the struggle of the people of El Salvador for justice and liberation has been an extremely important part of my personal and professional work— both at the Center for New Creation and for the Maryknoll Society. Since 1980 I have traveled to El Salvador many times; each time I am more deeply touched by the faith and commitment of the people I meet. The experience of accompanying some of these people, sometimes literally, as they returned to lands they had been forced to abandon, and of being deported from El Salvador myself in the process; the hard work of changing United States policy in El Salvador from one of extremely destructive engagement with the repressive forces to one of cooperation with the peace process—a work that included numerous arrests for civil disobedience; and the pain of living with refugees as they tried to integrate into an unwelcoming North American society have changed my life.

Beyond that, the witness of the many martyrs of El Salvador has profoundly shaped my spirituality. Foremost among them is Archbishop Oscar Romero. His sense of an appropriate role for the Church in the midst of horrific conflict, the radical and courageous nature of his commitment to the gospel and his openness to a God present among the poorest people and their communities have guided my own attempt at faithfulness. Few holy places have moved me as deeply as did the yet-unfinished cathedral in San Salvador where the simple tomb of the martyred archbishop remains, even a decade after his death, a haven for the people he loved so well.

Though Dorothy Day's life was much closer to mine geographically, she has been a much more distant figure in many ways. The research for this book, however, brought me into close contact with her life—even reintroduced me to her—and the gift of that encounter has been extraordinary. I have found in her an inspiring role model and an accessible friend.

Over the years I have known and been challenged by the Catholic Worker movement. Glimmers of Dorothy's values are reflected in my own life choices, especially in the decision to live in Assisi Community in an inner-city Washington, D.C., neighborhood. Most of my six children were raised or have lived for long periods of time in the community. Dorothy's own struggles to be at peace in an active, sometimes chaotic, always demanding community of people living together in less than ideal physical surroundings both inside and outside the community house have been consoling to me.

To discover that Dorothy Day herself chafed under the constraints of community life even as she celebrated that life and remained committed to it has given me strength to stay in a community I love and in which I deeply believe despite the frustrations. The fact that she was tormented with doubts about the impact of her life-style on her daughter calmed my own fears about the inadequacy of my own parenting, which has always been integrated with a commitment to the work for social justice—and in community for the last ten years. Her determination to find soul-space outside the oppressive urban center encouraged me to find a balance in my life that includes more time with the earth, a balance that has been lacking since we moved from our farm into the inner city ten years ago. The experience of poverty in our neighborhood is in many ways a gift to someone who never had to live in want, but Dorothy's example is impetus for me to find a bit of rural space to nurture our spirits as well.

Finally, Dorothy's deep belief in the value of "the little way" has given me strength to keep on keeping on after twenty-five years of working in the movement for peace and social justice. She has convinced me that the value is in the faithful doing day by day, in the transformation that happens as we walk on the margins and in the soul-deep knowledge that we are part of the communion of saints (among them Dorothy and Oscar) who have led the way to the New Creation.

In writing this retreat book with its conversations between Dorothy and Oscar, I have been aware that both spoke and wrote clearly and prolifically. I have tried to be faithful to each one's manner of expression and have used direct quotes whenever possible and appropriate within the dialogue itself. I hope that neither the insertion of many such quotes nor my own idea of a conversation between the two will distract.

I am grateful to Gloria Hutchinson for inviting me to participate in this retreat series. The process of doing so has been pure gift.

I am also grateful for the advice of Robert Ellsberg, editor-in-chief of Maryknoll's Orbis Books, whose expertise on the life of Dorothy Day helped me in my attempt to represent her ideas with authenticity. I am grateful for the assistance of Eugene Palumbo, a journalist friend whose life and work have for years been committed to the people of El Salvador. Finally, I am grateful to my friend Joseph Nangle, O.F.M., whose support and critique, rooted in years of experience in Latin America and a deep commitment to social justice, were invaluable as the book began to take shape.

Marie Adele Dennis

Introducing A Retreat With...

Twenty years ago I made a weekend retreat at a
Franciscan house on the coast of New Hampshire. The
retreat director's opening talk was as lively as a long-
range weather forecast. He told us how completely God
loves each one of us—without benefit of lively anecdotes
or fresh insights.

As the friar rambled on, my inner critic kept up a
sotto voce commentary: "I've heard all this before." "Wish
he'd say something new that I could chew on." "That poor
man really doesn't have much to say." Ever hungry for
manna yet untasted, I devalued any experience of hearing
the same old thing.

After a good night's sleep, I awoke feeling as peaceful
as a traveler who has at last arrived safely home. I walked
across the room toward the closet. On the way I passed
the sink with its small framed mirror on the wall above.
Something caught my eye like an unexpected presence. I
turned, saw the reflection in the mirror and said aloud,
"No wonder he loves me!"

This involuntary affirmation stunned me. What or
whom had I seen in the mirror? When I looked again, it
was "just me," an ordinary person with a lower-than-
average reservoir of self-esteem. But I knew that in the
initial vision I had seen God-in-me breaking through like a
sudden sunrise.

At that moment I knew what it meant to be made in
the divine image. I understood right down to my size

1

eleven feet what it meant to be loved exactly as I was. Only later did I connect this revelation with one granted to the Trappist monk-writer Thomas Merton. As he reports in *Conjectures of a Guilty Bystander*, while standing all unsuspecting on a street corner one day, he was overwhelmed by the "joy of being...a member of a race in which God Himself became incarnate.... There is no way of telling people that they are all walking around shining like the sun."

As an absentminded homemaker may leave a wedding ring on the kitchen windowsill, so I have often mislaid this precious conviction. But I have never forgotten that particular retreat. It persuaded me that the Spirit rushes in where it will. Not even a boring director or a judgmental retreatant can withstand the "violent wind" that "fills the entire house" where we dwell in expectation (see Acts 2:2).

So why deny ourselves any opportunity to come aside awhile and rest on holy ground? Why not withdraw from the daily web that keeps us muddled and wound? Wordsworth's complaint is ours as well: "The world is too much with us." There is no flu shot to protect us from infection by the skepticism of the media, the greed of commerce, the alienating influence of technology. We need retreats as the deer needs the running stream.

An Invitation

This book and its companions in the *A Retreat With...* series from St. Anthony Messenger Press are designed to meet that need. They are an invitation to choose as director some of the most powerful, appealing and wise mentors our faith tradition has to offer.

Our directors come from many countries, historical

eras and schools of spirituality. At times they are teamed to sing in close harmony (for example, Francis de Sales, Jane de Chantal and Aelred of Rievaulx on spiritual friendship). Others are paired to kindle an illuminating fire from the friction of their differing views (such as Augustine of Hippo and Mary Magdalene on human sexuality). All have been chosen because, in their humanness and their holiness, they can help us grow in self-knowledge, discernment of God's will and maturity in the Spirit.

Inviting us into relationship with these saints and holy ones are inspired authors from today's world, women and men whose creative gifts open our windows to the Spirit's flow. As a motto for the authors of our series, we have borrowed the advice of Dom Frederick Dunne to the young Thomas Merton. Upon joining the Trappist monks, Merton wanted to sacrifice his writing activities lest they interfere with his contemplative vocation. Dom Frederick wisely advised, "Keep on writing books that make people love the spiritual life."

That is our motto. Our purpose is to foster (or strengthen) friendships between readers and retreat directors—friendships that feed the soul with wisdom, past and present. Like the scribe "trained for the kingdom of heaven," each author brings forth from his or her storeroom "what is new and what is old" (Matthew 13:52).

The Format

The pattern for each *A Retreat With...* remains the same; readers of one will be in familiar territory when they move on to the next. Each book is organized as a seven-session retreat that readers may adapt to their own schedules or to the needs of a group.

Day One begins with an anecdotal introduction called "Getting to Know Our Directors." Readers are given a telling glimpse of the guides with whom they will be sharing the retreat experience. A second section, "Placing Our Directors in Context," will enable retreatants to see the guides in their own historical, geographical, cultural and spiritual settings.

Having made the human link between seeker and guide, the authors go on to "Introducing Our Retreat Theme." This section clarifies how the guide(s) are especially suited to explore the theme and how the retreatant's spirituality can be nourished by it.

After an original "Opening Prayer" to breathe life into the day's reflection, the author, speaking with and through the mentor(s), will begin to spin out the theme. While focusing on the guide(s)' own words and experience, the author may also draw on Scripture, tradition, literature, art, music, psychology or contemporary events to illuminate the path.

Each day's session is followed by reflection questions designed to challenge, affirm and guide the reader in integrating the theme into daily life. A "Closing Prayer" brings the session full circle and provides a spark of inspiration for the reader to harbor until the next session.

Days Two through Six begin with "Coming Together in the Spirit" and follow a format similar to Day One. Day Seven weaves the entire retreat together, encourages a continuation of the mentoring relationship and concludes with "Deepening Your Acquaintance," an envoi to live the theme by God's grace, the director(s)' guidance and the retreatant's discernment. A closing section of Resources serves as a larder from which readers may draw enriching books, videos, cassettes and films.

We hope readers will experience at least one of those memorable "No wonder God loves me!" moments. And we hope that they will have "talked back" to the mentors, as good friends are wont to do.

A case in point: There was once a famous preacher who always drew a capacity crowd to the cathedral. Whenever he spoke, an eccentric old woman sat in the front pew directly beneath the pulpit. She took every opportunity to mumble complaints and contradictions—just loud enough for the preacher to catch the drift that he was not as wonderful as he was reputed to be. Others seated down front glowered at the woman and tried to shush her. But she went right on needling the preacher to her heart's content.

When the old woman died, the congregation was astounded at the depth and sincerity of the preacher's grief. Asked why he was so bereft, he responded, "Now who will help me to grow?"

All of our mentors in *A Retreat With...* are worthy guides. Yet none would seek retreatants who simply said, "Where you lead, I will follow. You're the expert." In truth, our directors provide only half the retreat's content. Readers themselves will generate the other half.

As general editor for the retreat series, I pray that readers will, by their questions, comments, doubts and decision-making, fertilize the seeds our mentors have planted.

And may the Spirit of God rush in to give the growth.

Gloria Hutchinson
Series Editor
Conversion of Saint Paul, 1995

Getting to Know Our Directors

Introducing Dorothy Day (1897-1980)

From time to time a story gives privileged insight into the soul of another person, touching a quality of character that illuminates the whole. Such, I believe, is the "diamond story" about Dorothy Day told by a former member of the Catholic Worker staff, Tom Cornell:

> [A] well-dressed woman visited the Worker house one day and gave Dorothy a diamond ring.... Dorothy thanked the visitor, slipped the ring in her pocket, and later in the day gave it to an old woman who lived alone and often ate her meals at St. Joseph's. One of the staff protested to Dorothy that the ring could better have been sold at the Diamond Exchange and the money used to pay the woman's rent for a year. Dorothy replied that the woman had her dignity and could do as she liked with the ring. She could sell it for rent money or take a trip to the Bahamas. Or she could enjoy having a diamond ring on her hand just like the woman who had brought it to the Worker. "Do you suppose," Dorothy asked, "that God created diamonds only for the rich?"[1]

The life of Dorothy Day was in many ways an ordinary journey, but it was fired from the beginning with a passionate belief in the dignity of every human being and thereby transformed into one of the most important examples of gospel faithfulness in our times.

Dorothy was born in New York on November 8, 1897,

the third of five children in what would be a family of journalists and writers. John and Grace Satterlee Day moved their family to San Francisco, then Chicago and eventually back to New York. Theirs was a hard life, fluctuating from borderline poverty to a modicum of prosperity, depending on the status of John's employment.

Taking from her childhood seeds of concern about poverty and social injustice and a flickering attraction to the things of God, Dorothy crafted a career that embraced the wounds and wounded of her country in the tumultuous twentieth century. She was an active and increasingly visible figure from her earliest days as a young radical journalist in New York to the birth and nurturance of the Catholic Worker movement; from her many public actions of witness against injustice or violence to the raising of her strong, prophetic voice as conscience in the Catholic Church.

Dorothy's private life, like her more public journey, was engraved with the marks of a passionate seeker of life and love and deep human encounter. She seems to have nurtured always a deep and rich interior life. As a young woman she was profoundly affected by the writings of Dostoevsky and Tolstoy, Kropotkin and Upton Sinclair. From early sparks fanned by the good she saw in the lives of friends, and strengthened by her attraction to the Gospels and other inspirational literature, Dorothy also sought—and ultimately found—a place to meet God.

But early detours were excruciatingly painful. Between 1916 and 1918 she lived the bohemian life of a leftist journalist in New York. During this time she participated in a march for women's suffrage in Washington, D.C., and was arrested for the first time. Her weeks in jail in Occoquan, Virginia, were extremely difficult, albeit an experience of the suffering soul's yearning for God.

After a tragic affair ended in abortion and abandonment by the father of that child, Dorothy, married to a wealthy older man, left New York for Europe, where she wrote an autobiographical novel, *The Eleventh Virgin*. After her short-lived marriage ended in 1921, she returned to Chicago, the city of her childhood. Here she reentered the world of radical journalism and, gradually, healed her broken heart with the aid of the strength and compassion of friends. She was also nourished at that time by a reacquaintance with the most rejected human beings and sensed a gentle invitation to live in the presence of God. After some time working in New Orleans, Dorothy returned to New York in April 1924. As she reestablished old friendships, she purchased a cottage on Staten Island that would be a place of solitude and a writer's haven for years.

Soon Dorothy met and fell in love with Forster Batterham, an anarchist, atheist, humanist and naturalist, who returned her love but adamantly rejected marriage and religion as tyranny and opiate. Even as their love grew, the fire of Dorothy's faith in God burst into flame. The birth of their daughter, Tamar Teresa, in 1926 became the catalyst for her conversion to Roman Catholicism.

> No human creature could receive or contain so vast a flood of love and joy as I often felt after the birth of my child. With this came the need to worship, to adore.... My whole experience as a radical, my whole makeup, led me to want to associate with others, with the masses, in loving and praising God. Without even looking at the claims of the Catholic Church, I was willing to admit that for me she was the one true Church.... She claimed and held the allegiance of the masses of people in all the cities where I had lived. They poured in and out of her doors on Sundays and holy days.[2]

But her own choice for Baptism on December 28, 1927, was not easy. It signaled the end of her relationship with Forster, a relationship that had given Dorothy great joy and vitality. She also feared that by her Baptism she was abandoning the poor and betraying the radical movement for social justice of which she had been a part. Despite its appeal to the masses, the institutional Church was closely associated with money and power.

Dorothy redoubled her efforts to integrate her life in God and her passion for social justice. Soon she abandoned her Marxist affiliations in favor of nonviolent means to achieve a more just world and joined a religious pacifist organization, the Fellowship of Reconciliation. Still she wandered—to California and Mexico—in search of ways to survive with her daughter and to honor her own commitments, but the signs of the times were ominous. The Depression had begun to take its toll. Dorothy and Tamar Teresa returned to New York, where homelessness and hopelessness had become a way of life in some areas, and the burning question about how to respond pierced Dorothy's soul.

As a reporter for *Commonweal* and *America* magazines, Dorothy accompanied a hunger march from New York to Washington late in 1930, but was deeply saddened by the fact that it was organized by communists, not Christians. She prayed in the crypt at the unfinished Shrine of the Immaculate Conception at Catholic University to find a path that would enable her to work for social change as a Catholic Christian.

Waiting for her and her child upon her return to New York was Peter Maurin, a Frenchman of Franciscan bent whose idea of a new social order intrigued Dorothy. Dorothy's energy, talent and experience and Peter Maurin's ideas joined in the publication of a new radical Catholic newspaper, a voice for social justice and a new way of peaceful social transformation. The first edition of *The Catholic Worker* was on the streets of New York on May 1, 1930. From the beginning, Peter was adamant that the new journal should announce the vision of new community, both urban and rural, as well as denounce the injustice and oppression so evident all around. Soon the vision began to blossom for Dorothy, Peter and the community formed around them. Hospitality became a way of life. The foundations of this new Catholic Worker movement, this revolutionary and rooted life-style, were Christian community, respect for the dignity of the individual and the importance of individual action for social justice, pacifism, nonviolence and voluntary poverty.

Under her strong leadership *The Catholic Worker* denounced the anti-Semitism rearing its ugly head in the 1930's and, on grounds of pacifism a few years later, opposed World War II. It criticized the internment by the United States government of Japanese Americans in the name of national security and decried the abomination of atomic bombs unleashed in the name of peace. Catholic Workers refused to participate in the draft or civil defense preparedness schemes. Theirs were among the first voices opposing United States engagement in Korea and Vietnam.

Dorothy Day lived for the remainder of her long life rested in what seemed to be a profound integration of heart and soul, faith and good works, commitment to social justice and life in God. Dorothy was mother, sister, companion; worker, journalist, inspiration; radical activist and prophet. She relentlessly pursued the roots of injustice and violence and confronted the powerful in Church and State to do the same. She walked on picket lines and went to jail as a result. Dorothy Day loved deeply and personally; she saw the world through the eyes of those who were poor because she lived in community with them. By their measure she measured her own faithfulness and that of the society in which she lived.

Introducing Oscar Romero (1917-1980)

The story of Oscar Romero, Archbishop of San Salvador, El Salvador, is the story of a courageous and faith-filled people who drew out of a conservative hierarch a commitment to live in the footsteps of Christ. As he walked deliberately into the jaws of the hellish violence that held sway in his beloved homeland, Romero knew that his life was in danger. He knew as well that the roots and the fruit of his own life were in the poor community that he had come to love and to call his own. "If they kill me," he said in words that have now become familiar around the world, "I will rise again in the Salvadoran people." And he has.

Oscar Romero was born in Ciudad Barrios, San Miguel, in the eastern part of El Salvador on August 15, 1917. His early years were marked by the steady pace and hard work of a family living with very few amenities. He had a simple education in a poor school until he was a young teenager, then an apprenticeship with a local carpenter. But prayer had apparently become a major force in his young life and a decision to go to the seminary seemed a natural, if major, step into the unknown. Little did anyone know what a fateful step that was—what a work of the Spirit it would turn out to be!

After studies in San Miguel and San Salvador and ordination in Rome on April 4, 1942, World War II forced Oscar to abandon his doctoral studies and return to El Salvador. Soon he was immersed in the work of the Church. In addition to his pastoral work, he served the

San Miguel diocese as secretary, high school chaplain and journalist. He was a fine preacher, careful to connect his message with the daily experiences of the faithful people who listened. "The kingdom of heaven begins right here," he would say.[3]

Winds of change from the Second Vatican Council were not at first welcomed by Oscar. In 1967 he took up a new position as secretary-general of the Salvadoran Bishops' Conference; soon after he was named executive secretary of the Central American Bishops' Conference and an auxiliary bishop in San Salvador. He accepted each new responsibility with energy, commitment and with a conservative mind-set. Exceptionally troublesome for him at first were the words spoken at Medellin, Colombia, in 1968, when the Latin American Conference of Bishops articulated a fundamentally new posture for their Church. Flowing from the movement of the Spirit at the Vatican Council and responding to an impoverished world, the message of Medellin reoriented the Latin American Catholic Church to the side of the poor and oppressed— especially those who suffered institutional violence. The consequences were earth-shattering for those who understood the gospel message as one of peace and reconciliation. The pursuit of social justice and liberation too often seemed to lead to division and conflict.

In 1971 Oscar became editor of the diocesan newspaper, *Orientacion*. In that and subsequent positions in the archdiocese, including rector of the diocesan seminary, he was an active participant in some of the most controversial events in a tumultous era for the Salvadoran Church. Although widely considered cautious and conservative, Romero was at all times a faithful and prayerful son of Holy Mother Church. For years he clung to his belief in the basic goodness of those who were in power in El Salvador and was disturbed by the activities of those who were calling for an end to the social, political and economic status quo. In particular he was opposed to the involvement of priests, religious and Catholic communities in such a struggle, though, as James Brockman writes, he was "blind to his own political stance in support of the government while worrying about the 'politicization' of those who dared to question those in power."[4] He was always worried that the liberation desired would be only material in nature, that the need for spiritual liberation would be forgotten.

In 1974 Romero was named bishop of Santiago de Maria. There, as official repression against the rural poor began to escalate and massacres became too common and too close to home, he was faced with an unavoidable challenge to speak out against the violence. At first he did so privately and politely, assuming that the killings were an aberration, not government policy, and that they would be stopped once official El Salvador knew what was happening.

He was profoundly affected by the suffering of the poor, especially by the plight of those who worked on coffee plantations in his diocese. He opened the rectory and diocesan buildings to shelter them; he condemned the injustice with which they were treated. Slowly, the impoverished and violated people of his diocese led their shepherd to a better understanding of the reality they lived. Moved by compassion, Oscar began to feel the fire of righteous anger stir in his soul. He began to distance himself from the powerful ones who maintained the system intact. He began to understand that transformation of Salvadoran society could not be accomplished without conflict and that his association with the political and military leaders and economic elites on whose behalf the system worked gave unspoken assent to the injustice and repression that kept them in power.

In February 1977 Oscar Arnulfo Romero was installed as archbishop of San Salvador, just as the brutal forces of repression in El Salvador turned their attention to a Church that was publicly defending the rights of campesinos to organize and to demand justice. The unequal distribution of land had long fueled the fires of injustice in El Salvador. When even a feeble attempt at land reform floundered at the hands of wealthy landowners, the Church intensified its work in defense of the landless poor. Some foreign priests were deported; Salvadoran priests were threatened. At the same time, other tensions in El Salvador were increasing, sparked by a fraudulent election and culminating in the brutal massacre of demonstrators in Plaza Libertad in San Salvador.

Oscar had come a long way toward confronting the blatant injustice in El Salvador, but the assassination of his dear friend, Rutillo Grande, S.J., with two campesinos on March 12, 1977, is generally thought to have been the point of no return. Pastor at Aguilares (north of San Salvador), Rutillo had been working in a rural community with a team of Jesuits for several years. Their efforts to animate "delegates of the Word" in the community and their support of the campesinos' most basic rights evoked the fury of landowners.

For the next three years, until his own assassination during a celebration of the Eucharist on March 24, 1980, Oscar Romero was an untiring and outspoken advocate of the most marginal and oppressed among the Salvadoran people. His close association with a people struggling for a measure of social justice clearly shaped his life. He denounced injustice with unwavering clarity, but always with love. He agonized over the hardness of heart that prevailed among the powerful of El Salvador. He cried out for an end to United States support for the forces of repression. He pleaded with the military to stop the killing. He guided the Church on a fine line between disengagement and partisan activity. He was a prophet in the most classical sense. And he gave his life for it.

Placing Our Directors in Context

Although they were contemporaries concerned with the same issues of justice and peace, the worlds of Oscar Romero and Dorothy Day were light years apart.

Dorothy's World

Dorothy's world was that of the twentieth-century United States—the "War to End All Wars" (World War I), the Roaring Twenties, the Great Depression—a world of rapid change. During her youth, United States Marines landed in Honduras, Cuba, Nicaragua, Santo Domingo and Haiti; relations with Mexico grew extremely tense and, after years of resistance, the United States joined the Allied Forces in fighting on the European front.

At the same time labor organizing and radical politics caught the nation's attention. Textile workers struck plants in Lawrence, Massachusetts, in 1912; Ford Motor Company invented the assembly line in 1913 and a wave of strikes in 1919 gave rise to the the Red scare. Workers also accomplished important gains in Dorothy's early years, including the five-day work week and the eight-hour day.

As Dorothy entered adulthood, the Russian Revolution was headline news and the American Communist Party was being organized in Chicago. Thousands of immigrants and radicals were arrested and deported from the United States. Sacco and Vanzetti were arrested and finally executed in Massachusetts despite international protests. During these years, racial tensions were heightened in the United States. The Ku Klux Klan spread terror in the South, and open conflict erupted in many cities, including Washington, D.C., East St. Louis, Chicago, Detroit and New York.

During the 1920's women finally won the right to vote and prohibition was enacted. Automobiles, radio and feature-length movies became popular. But following Black Tuesday, October 29, 1929, when the stock market crashed and the Great Depression began, banks, businesses and farms failed across the country. A certain prosperity and optimism gave way to widespread poverty, unemployment and insecurity. The United States declared a moratorium on international debt and war reparations payments. Within three years, the stock market had dropped to ten percent of its 1929 value and national income was cut in half. In an attempt at recovery, President Franklin Delano Roosevelt instituted the controversial New Deal, including the Wagner Act to protect unions, the Social Security Act and the Wealth Tax Act.

As signs of war became more evident during the 1930's, the United States moved from repeated declarations of neutrality to "non-belligerency" and finally to a declaration of war in 1941. World War II formed the context for Dorothy's clearly articulated radical pacifism. She lived in the country that developed and used atomic bombs. She watched the nuclear age and the Cold War unfold and she refused at all times to participate in the relentless march toward annihilation. In the process, she saw an antiwar movement grow from an extremely unpopular minority during World War II to a formidable public force during the Vietnam War.

Dorothy lived through the Depression, the New Deal,

the Second World War, the Korean War, the McCarthy Era, the civil rights and Black nationalist movements, the beginning of the space age, the Cuban Revolution and the backlash it evoked in the United States, the assassinations of John and Robert Kennedy and Martin Luther King, Jr., the turbulent 1960's and 1970's. Through it all, she deliberately located herself with the most excluded people. She lived through at least two eras of visible radical dissent in the United States, the 1920's and the 1960's, and actively participated in the best of both. She saw prosperity return to the United States in the 1950's and advocated voluntary poverty as consumerism and the worst sort of materialism gripped our society. She planted seeds for and saw the War on Poverty grow.

She saw repeated struggles for labor justice, from longshoremen and grave-diggers to the United Farm Workers of America. She fed New York strikers and fasted with Cesar Chavez. She saw powerful labor unions articulate a clear agenda for their workers, and watched as corruption and greed seeped into the movement.

After her conversion in the mid 1920's, Dorothy's was a Catholic world as well. The Church she chose was one of rigid, traditional teachings and a fear of the "secular," but it claimed a rich sacramental life and more and more clearly articulated social teaching. The Second Vatican Council dramatically changed the relationship of the Church and the world; the years immediately following the Council saw an even more urgent social message emerge. Dorothy and the Catholic Worker movement helped forge the way for lay leadership of the Church in the modern world.

Oscar's World

Oscar's world was that of twentieth-century El

Salvador. He was born during the First World War, but the struggles in his homeland were very far—perhaps centuries—away from D-Day or the Battle of the Bulge. His was the world of the rural poor in a small country where the wealthiest "fourteen families" controlled all the economic and political power. As a child he lived where education and modern health care were unaffordable luxuries for most people—where running water, plumbing and telephones were rare. His was a polarized world with a status quo defined by inequality.

During his lifetime, and especially during the years of his priestly ministry, Oscar witnessed great changes in the Latin American Catholic Church, including the Church in El Salvador, as well as in Salvadoran society. He was ordained in a pre-Vatican II Church and walked with the Latin American Church as it articulated its own response to the Council.

In the aftermath of the landmark Medellin meeting, many pastoral workers moved into the barrios or neighborhoods of Latin America to experience and to try to understand the lives of the poor. The process of liberation theology in these marginal but organized communities was important in those years. No longer did the Church preach acceptance of and submission to authority with assurances of great rewards in heaven for those who suffered on earth. Rather, the communities (often called Christian base communities) were encouraged to reflect on the message of Jesus out of the miserable context of their own lives. A pastoral process of integrating reflection on the word of God with action for social justice to make the world more consistent with the gospel vision was developed and widely used.

In El Salvador this community-based model of Catholic action for social change had a tremendous impact. Poor Christian communities began to see that the demands of their faith could lead them to join with other popular social groups working for a change in the status quo. As the clamor for justice in El Salvador strengthened, reaction from the people in power and their allies was fierce. The 1970's and 1980's saw a turn for the worse. Official security forces (the Salvadoran army and police) and right-wing death squads mounted a vicious attack on anyone suspected of participating in the call for social transformation. Repeated attempts to resolve the deepening conflict through political means or negotiation rapidly disintegrated. Promises of land reform or respect for human rights were empty.

As tensions grew, the United States became more and more deeply involved. Fearing a spread of communism in the hemisphere and the success of a popular revolution, the United States gave substantial support to the military and conservative political forces. After the victorious Sandinista revolution in Nicaragua in July 1979, the United States government became even more frightened. By the late 1980's, it was sending one and a half million dollars per day to El Salvador to help crush the popular revolutionary movement there.

Repression against any popular organization and very specifically against the Church—base communities and pastoral workers—was already intense when Romero was made Archbishop of San Salvador in 1977. Torture, disappearance, kidnapping and extrajudicial executions became commonplace—mostly perpetrated by official forces and their cohorts.

Within weeks after Romero became archbishop, his Jesuit friend Rutillo Grande and two companions were assassinated. Security forces opened fire at two public demonstrations in San Salvador (February 28 in the Plaza Libertad and May 1 at Parque Cuscatlan). Within months, scores of pastoral agents and several other priests, including Alfonso Navarro, were killed by death squads. In 1978 and 1979 the repression intensified. Father Ernesto Barrera was killed; Father Octavio Ortiz and four young people on a retreat with him were massacred; Father Rafael Palacios and Father Alirio Napoleon Macias were murdered. Whole villages fled from rural areas into the city for refuge. Thousands of people left El Salvador for other countries.

Archbishop Romero was formed by the reality he saw, by the horror, the violence, the brutality, the injustice he witnessed. He had to speak out. More and more surely he demanded an end to the repression. More and more confidently he spoke words of hope into the violence.

Oscar Romero was killed on March 24, 1980. The war in El Salvador raged for twelve more years, claiming the lives of over seventy thousand civilians, mostly poor people. On December 2, 1980, the day his companion on this retreat, Dorothy Day, was buried in New York, four churchwomen from the United States—Maura Clarke, M.M., Ita Ford, M.M., Dorothy Kazel, O.S.U., and Jean Donovan—joined the ranks of the martyrs in El Salvador and bound in new ways the people yearning for peace with justice in two lands.

Notes

1 Jim Forest, *Love Is the Measure: A Biography of Dorothy Day* (Maryknoll, N.Y.: Orbis Books, 1986, 1994), pp. 90-91.

2 Ibid, pp. 63-64.

3 James R. Brockman, S.J., *The Word Remains: A Life of Oscar Romero* (Maryknoll, N.Y.: Orbis, 1982), p. 35.

4 Ibid, p. 49.

DAY ONE

Conversion: Seeing With New Eyes

Introducing Our Retreat Theme

Dorothy Day and Oscar Romero are well known to people of faith concerned about poverty and social justice in the modern world. Their journeys suggest to us that when life is seen through the eyes of poor people and lived in response to that vision, a rich spirituality and serious engagement in social transformation may result. As he allowed the reality of poverty and injustice to challenge his assumptions about life, Oscar began to see that a gospel-shaped response to concrete political, social and economic realities was a necessary companion to life in the Spirit. As Dorothy walked in the shoes of her poor friends, she sought a life in the Spirit to accompany her commitment to social change. Both opened their eyes to see the reality of poverty and allowed that sight to change their lives. Both experienced the importance of community in support of the discipleship journey. The gospel and the witness of these saints invite us to do the same.

Opening Prayer

O LORD, you have searched me and known me.
You know when I sit down and when I rise up;
  you discern my thoughts from far away.
You search out my path and my lying down,
  and are acquainted with all my ways.[1]

Holy One, Hound of Heaven,
be with me on the journey of this retreat.
Spirit of Life, Enduring Gift,
pour forth your wisdom.
Grant me understanding;
gift me with knowledge
that I may know and follow you.

Search me, O God, and know my heart;
  test me and know my thoughts.
See if there is any wicked way in me,
  and lead me in the way everlasting.[2]

Glory to you, Source of all being,
Eternal Word and Holy Spirit,
as it was in the beginning,
is now and will be forever. Amen.

Scripture

They came to Bethsaida. Some people brought a
blind man to him and begged him to touch him. He
took the blind man by the hand and led him out of
the village; and when he had put saliva on his eyes
and laid his hands on him, he asked him, "Can you
see anything?" And the man looked up and said, "I
can see people, but they look like trees, walking."
Then Jesus laid his hands on his eyes again; and he

looked intently and his sight was restored, and he saw everything clearly. Then he sent him away to his home, saying, "Do not even go into the village."[3]

RETREAT SESSION ONE

The Conversation Begins

It is the year 1980. A young-at-heart old woman and a slightly younger old man sit for some hours of conversation. Years of struggle have brought clarity to the vision of each. Despite evidence of a deep weariness, each has placed a passionate claim on life. Their conversation ranges widely. Each reviews an individual journey with God that was shaped by their times. They lived in different worlds, yet their paths were much alike.

Dorothy: It was the poor people.

Oscar: The poor ones.

Dorothy: Injustice and oppression.

Oscar: Neglect, a lack of charity.

But among the poorest people and their communities, both found life. As a young child Dorothy apparently had encountered God. She writes of moments when she was aware of God's presence—when she tasted the delight of God's embrace. But as a young woman in Chicago, Dorothy also began to look with care at the reality of her world. Writers like the Russian revolutionary Peter Kropotkin and American novelist and reformer Upton

Sinclair reached her heart.

Dorothy:

> When what I read made me particularly class
> conscious, I used to turn from the park with all its
> beauty and peacefulness and walk down to North
> Avenue and over west through slum districts, and
> watch the slatternly women and the unkempt
> children and ponder over the poverty of the homes
> as contrasted with the wealth along the shore drive. I
> wanted even then to play my part. I wanted to write
> such books that thousands upon thousands of
> readers would be convinced of the injustice of things
> as they were.[4]

I could not stand the great gap between their lives and
mine. Their suffering touched me. Social injustice, the
festering roots of poverty, infuriated me. But I began to
seek a solution in radical politics, not radical faith. I tried
to shed a religion that accepted an unjust social order. I
walked away from a Christ I thought was dead.

Oscar: I was born poor and loved the simple communities
of my poor Salvadoran homeland. I was always kind and
generous to those who suffered, especially after I followed
God's call and was ordained a priest. But I assumed that
poverty was part of the plan of God. At first I did not see
its roots in social injustice.

Dorothy: As a journalist I wrote about and supported the
revolutionary thinking of the left. My friends were
communists and anarchists and workers demanding their
rights. I was intent on waking up or overturning a status
quo that was harmful to poor people.

Oscar: As a priest, even though I cared about those who were poor, I sought harmony and stability, with charity to moderate the status quo and alleviate suffering. I so clearly remember saying how beautiful it would be in El Salvador if

> we should bear in our souls the resolve to understand one another better, each one in the place where the hand of Providence has put him; if the members of the government and the shepherds of the church, if capital and labor, if those of the city and those of the country, the initiatives of the government and those of private enterprise—all of us, were to really let the divine Savior of the world, patron of the nation, inspire and mediate all our conflicts and be the artisan of all the national transformations that we urgently need for the integral liberation that only he can build.[5]

Dorothy: I loved life and lived it fully, I thought. I was writing about social struggles and injustice and I loved to probe the minds of the most radical intellectuals in New York City.

Oscar: For a long time, I was worried that the radicals in my country would create a godless society. I was afraid of the revolution I saw coming. You and I, Dorothy, would have had little in common then, I'm afraid! But when I was bishop of Santiago de Maria, I was shocked to discover that the plantation owners were only paying their workers a portion of the minimum wage—far less than they needed to survive. Many of the landowners were Catholic people. I knew them well. But I also knew the workers and saw how hard life was for them. Their plight began to gnaw at my soul. I began to see with new eyes what was happening. I began to hear in a new way what my priests closest to the poor were saying. I had intended to close the Passionists' Center for Education—it was teaching about liberation and I feared it had lost a sense of God's Reign as transcendent. I changed my mind.

Dorothy: We really were in different places! I left behind a religion that I thought cared only about the hereafter, not the here and now! But slowly, slowly my eyes were opened as well. I remember the story that Grushenka tells in *The Brothers Karamazov* about the woman whose guardian angel could not rescue her from hell. One time in her life of evil the woman had pulled an onion and given it to a beggar. So God gave her one chance to be pulled out of the eternal fire by holding onto an onion. When other sinners tried to save themselves by grabbing onto her, she pushed them back. The onion broke, and all were lost.

> Sometimes in thinking and wondering at God's goodness to me, I have thought that it was because I gave away an onion. Because I sincerely loved His poor, He taught me to know Him.... But always the glimpses of God most came when I was alone.... It was in those few years that I found Him. I found Him at last through joy and thanksgiving, not through sorrow. Yet, how can I say that either? Better let it be said that I found Him through His poor, and in a moment of joy I turned to Him. I have said, sometimes flippantly, that the mass of bourgeois smug Christians who denied Christ in His poor made me turn to Communism, and that it was the Communists and working with them that made me turn to God....[6]

Oscar: I remember the shift that took place in my own process for evaluating a given situation, my own method of discerning the way of the Spirit.

For many years, I studied the word of God in the abstract. I defined faithfulness as obedience to the universal Church. My relationship with God was personal and very important to me—a guide and source of strength for my life. It still is. But these years of conflict in El Salvador and the terrible suffering that is root and result of the violence have forced me to open my eyes.

Dorothy: What I discovered as I probed the painful reality around me, but also as I reveled in the beauty of nature—as I made space in my soul—what I discovered was the God I could not find before. Working to change the injustices of society was working for and with this God. This God is among the poor, the prisoner, the stranger.

Oscar: Yes, God was always a part of my life, a central part of my life, but faithfulness to that God and to the pursuit of life eternal became more and more intertwined with the building of a new society here on earth—for me, specifically in El Salvador.

Dorothy: For me, at first, in the United States—but way beyond that as well.

Oscar: I began to see that I would have to choose the side of the poor ones, but I think I underestimated the cost.

For Reflection

We do not have to look very far these days to encounter poverty; people in great numbers still live on the margins. According to the United Nations Development Program (UNDP) 1996 Human Development Report, more than one billion people lack access to basic health care and education, safe drinking water and adequate nutrition. About one in three people live in poverty. Even in wealthier countries, more than a hundred million people live below the official poverty line and five million are homeless.

Wrapped inside these statistics are human beings and their communities—people impoverished by a system that does not work to their benefit. These people are or ought to be our neighbors, our loved ones, our honored guests. At least we ought to see with new eyes the reality in which they live. The gospel calls us to "look intensely" so that we may see clearly and act in response.

- *Take some time to think through the routine of your day, your life. In what ways might you be blind?*

- *Where do you see poverty? Can people be outcasts even if they are not economically poor? Are you yourself an outcast?*

- *How do you interact with those on the margins? Does the reality of life on the margins have any impact on your worldview? Your politics? Your actions? What is the connection for you between life in God and work for a just social order and the New Creation?*

Closing Prayer

Search me, O God, and know my heart;
Open my eyes to see clearly this world of ours.
Give me the courage to look at the pain and injustice.
Help me as well to see the hope,
and grant me the grace to respond in your name.[7]

Glory to you, Source of All Being,
Eternal Word and Holy Spirit,

as it was in the beginning,
is now and will be forever.
Amen.

Notes

[1] Psalm 139:1-3.

[2] Psalm 139:23-24.

[3] Mark 8:22-26.

[4] *Dorothy Day, Selected Writings: By Little and By Little,* ed. Robert Ellsberg (Maryknoll, N.Y.: Orbis Books, 1992), p. 13. Originally published in 1983 by Alfred A. Knopf as *By Little and By Little: The Selected Writings of Dorothy Day.*

[5] James R. Brockman, S.J., *The Word Remains: A Life of Oscar Romero,* p. 51.

[6] *Selected Writings,* pp. 6, 7.

[7] See Psalm 139:23-24.

DAY TWO
Accompaniment:
Barrios and Breadlines

Coming Together in the Spirit

> The mystery of the poor is this: that they are Jesus,
> and what you do for them you do for Him. It is the
> only way we have of knowing and believing in our
> love. The mystery of poverty is that by sharing in it,
> making ourselves poor in giving to others, we
> increase our knowledge of and belief in love.[1]

Defining Our Thematic Context

Two souls, Dorothy and Oscar, made very different,
but equally profound decisions. Each chose to walk in a
new direction, to follow an invitation of the Spirit. Neither
could have known the ultimate consequences of this step.
For these two faithful people it was simply the next step—
like so many of our own. Each had an insight, an
inclination toward life in the God of the Poor.

For Oscar, conversion required relocation—a
deliberate following of the Spirit to the side of poor
communities in a situation of painful social conflict. He
saw with new eyes the action of a God he already knew
and loved on behalf of the marginal, the excluded ones of

his day. New life in the God of the Poor meant a new way of being in relationship with poor people.

For Dorothy, conversion also required relocation, a new relationship, a move toward the God she had left behind but inevitably encountered again dwelling with the excluded ones at whose side she had already decided to live and struggle.

The poor barrios of El Salvador would become the guide and life's blood for Oscar's ministry of social justice in a cruelly unjust society. The breadlines of New York would become Dorothy's impetus toward and the place where she encountered God.

Though in vastly different worlds, the common denominator was their commitment to walk with God, accompanying impoverished and marginalized people in pursuit of life.

Opening Prayer

We see you, God,
in the barrios and breadlines of our world.
Open our hearts to encounter you in love there.
Fill us with the desire to be near you,
broken but whole,
illiterate but wise beyond measure.

Shape us, mold us,
guide us, lead us
to be at your side and theirs.

Scripture

As he was setting out on a journey, a man ran up and
knelt before him, and asked him, "Good Teacher,
what must I do to inherit eternal life?" Jesus said to
him, "Why do you call me good? No one is good but
God alone. You know the commandments: 'You shall
not murder; You shall not commit adultery; You shall
not steal; You shall not bear false witness; You shall
not defraud; Honor your father and mother.'" He
said to him, "Teacher, I have kept all these since my
youth." Jesus, looking at him, loved him and said,
"You lack one thing; go, sell what you own, and give
the money to the poor, and you will have treasure in
heaven; then come, follow me." When he heard this,
he was shocked and went away grieving, for he had
many possessions.[2]

Retreat Session Two

Oscar: As I tried to sort out the most difficult questions—
how to respond to escalating repression against people
and a Church that stood with them, a Church of the
people—I began to seek the counsel of poor people and of
those pastoral workers who were closest to them. It
became clearer and clearer to me that the harmony I
treasured was an illusion shattered by injustice. I was
adamantly opposed to the use of the Church for
ideological purposes and felt the need to be more
grounded in the experience of poor communities—more in
touch with their view of the world. I wanted to get
beneath the ideology, to understand what was at the heart
of the conflict. Often just listening to campesinos tell their
stories gave me both courage and clarity. I would always

give preference to them—even if others had to wait. I
remember saying,

> I have my priorities. With or without a schedule I am
> always going to receive first any campesino who
> arrives here—whatever day or hour that might be,
> and whether or not I am in a meeting.... My brother
> bishops all have cars; pastors can take a bus and not
> have huge problems waiting. But campesinos walk
> long distances and face many dangers. Often they
> have not eaten. Even yesterday one came from La
> Union. He had been hit very hard on the nape of his
> neck by a National Guard soldier and blinded. He
> only came to tell me the story.... The campesinos
> never ask me for anything. They only tell me what is
> on their mind and are thus relieved.[3]

Dorothy: What a privileged place it is alongside the
broken and the brokenhearted! I, too, am forever amazed
by the clarity of their vision and changed by the deep faith
I so often witness in their lives. But Jesus' words to the
rich young man are very difficult to understand and even
harder to follow. As long as we ourselves are insulated by
comfort, we lose sight of the *burden* of poverty, we forget
about the *causes* of poverty and we will never own our
own role *in creating* poverty. Even when we have been
given the gift of sight, to see the reality of injustice in our
world, we will become blind again very quickly if we
don't literally accompany those living in poverty day after
endless day. Maybe we are afraid to pray for the grace to
accompany the poor ones, "yet I am convinced that it is
the grace we most need in this age of crisis."[4]

Oscar: My friend Rutillo was always on my mind. He
accompanied well the campesinos of Aguilares. His
wisdom was rooted in his life with them. The truth he

spoke was shaped by the reality of their lives. Listen to the words of a campesino who attended to his body:

> When I heard the news, I felt like I'd been hurled into the air and then fallen to the ground. I was so distraught, I don't even know how I got to the church. It's only now that I'm asking myself how I managed to live through everything that happened that day.
>
> I received Father Grande's body, and helped to undress him. I took off his socks; they were soaked with blood.
>
> I loved him. That's why I took a piece of cloth caked with his blood. I'll keep it forever.
>
> The priests gave me permission to be at the parish for the two nights of the wake. We all gathered there and spent those nights recalling the great Christian communities we had built with him.
>
> The first night, at midnight, Archbishop Romero arrived. He walked up to the little table where we had placed Father Grande's body. He was wrapped in a white sheet. You could tell from the way the archbishop looked at him how much he loved him, too.
>
> We hadn't known Archbishop Romero until that night, and we had never heard him preach. The big surprise hit us as we listened to him. We all said the same thing: "He sounds just like Father Grande."
>
> It seemed to us that right there Father Grande's message passed on to Archbishop Romero. Really, right there. I whispered to one of my friends, "Could it be that God has worked this miracle so that we won't be left as orphans?"[5]

Dorothy: Yes, the voice of the poor carries authenticity. We who live in the United States live in luxury compared to people in many other parts of the world—like your El Salvador, my friend. Even our destitute are affected by this wealth. Sometimes they partake in it; at other times it is a temptation and an affront to their humanity. But the question we must always ask ourselves—we who are forever privileged through nutrition and health care and education—is whether our wealth is gained from their poverty. If so, accompanying the poor, sharing their lot is not an option, but an obligation.

In my country I often tell the following story. It is the story of Saint Ignatius of Sardinia, a Capuchin friar who used to go out from his monastery with a sack to beg from the people of the town, but who would never go to a merchant who had built up his fortune by defrauding the poor.

> Franchino, the rich man, fumed every time the saint passed his door. His concern, however, was not the loss of the opportunity to give alms, but fear of public opinion. He complained at the friary, whereupon the Father Guardian ordered St. Ignatius to beg from the merchant the next time he went out.
>
> "Very well," said Ignatius, obediently. "If you wish it, Father, I will go, but I would not have the Capuchins dine on the blood of the poor...." The merchant received Ignatius with great flattery and gave him generous alms, asking him to come again in the future. But hardly had Ignatius left the house with his sack on his shoulder when drops of blood began oozing from the sack. They trickled down on Franchino's doorstep and ran down through the street to the monastery. Everywhere Ignatius went, a trickle of blood followed him. When he arrived at the friary, he laid the sack at the Father Guardian's feet. "What is this?" gasped the Guardian. "This," St. Ignatius said, "is the blood of the poor."[6]

Oscar: What we developed as we walked with poor people—campesinos, the homeless, the urban poor—was a new awareness of injustice and a passionate commitment to social transformation. What we encountered was real life—raw, painful, beautiful, sometimes ugly—but real. My commitment to accompaniment brought me quickly and consciously to places of horrendous violence and conflict. Such was the reality of El Salvador in my day. I found myself in places I hoped I would never be: comforting families as they viewed the butchered remains of loved ones in ditches and morgues; gathering in my arms refugees exhausted by days in flight from the military without food or shelter; huddled under plastic on the grounds of the seminary; praying over the remains of murdered priests and pastoral workers—martyrs for justice in our land.

Dorothy: My commitment to accompaniment—my letting go in order to walk with the most marginal—was also extremely difficult, but my agony at times was much more private. At times I was particularly concerned about my daughter, Tamar Teresa. Once I wrote,

> the little time I have with her, being constantly on the go, having to leave her in the care of others, sending her away to school so that she can lead a regular life and not be subject to the moods and vagaries of the crowd of us! This is probably the cruelest hardship of all. She is happy, she does not feel torn constantly as I do. And then the doubt arises, probably she too feels that I am failing her.... Never before have I had such a complete sense of failure, of utter misery.[7]

For Reflection

The invitation to accompaniment is an invitation to let go of whatever barriers exist between ourselves and those on the margins, people in barrios and on breadlines. Accompaniment means eliminating from our lives whatever wealth or privilege we have acquired on the backs of the poor. According to Dorothy,

> It also means non-participation in those comforts and luxuries which have been manufactured by the exploitation of others.... If our jobs do not contribute to the common good, we pray God for the grace to give them up. Have they to do with shelter, food, clothing? Have they to do with the Works of Mercy? Everyone should be able to place his [or her] job in the category of the Works of Mercy.... Whatever has contributed to the misery and degradation of the poor may be considered a bad job, and not to be worked at....
>
> It means what Peter calls regional living. This means fasting from tea, coffee, grapefruit, pineapple, etc., from things not grown in the region in which one lives. One day last winter we bought broccoli which had the label on it of a corporation farm in Arizona or Texas, where we had seen men, women, and children working at two o'clock in the morning with miner's lamps on their foreheads to avoid the terrible heat of day. These were homeless migrants, of which there are some million in the United States. For these there is "no room in the inn."
>
> We ought not to eat food produced under such conditions. We ought not to smoke, not only because it is a useless habit, but also because tobacco impoverishes the soil and pauperizes the farmer, and means women and children working in the fields....
>
> [Accompanying those who are poor] means having a bare minimum in the way of clothes, and seeing to it that these are made under decent working conditions, proper wages and hours, etc. The union label tries to guarantee this....

[It] means not riding on rubber while horrible working conditions prevail in the rubber industry..., not riding on rails while bad conditions exist in the coal mines and steel mills..., not accepting that courteous bribe from the railroads, the clergy rate. Railroads have been built on robbery and exploitation.... Of course we are not all given the grace to do such things. But it is good to call to mind the vision.[8]

Read again Mark 10:17-22.

- *Dorothy calls poverty the "pearl of great price," something to be sought after. We usually read the story of the rich young man with some anxiety. What does it mean for you?*

- *Jesus invited the young man to leave behind whatever was holding him in bondage. It was a clear invitation to discipleship, a discipleship lived out at the margins of society where the Reign of God, the New Creation, a new society was being born. How can you accompany impoverished and marginalized people?*

- *How can you learn to live with the poor if you are not already doing so?*

- *What implications does this invitation have for your life-style? Your work? Your diet? Your recreation? The products you buy?*

Closing Prayer

Search me, O God, and know my heart,
    test me and know my thoughts.
See if there is any wicked way in me,
    and lead me in the way everlasting.[9]

Teach me how to accompany

the ones most marginalized in our times.
Let my heart
and my view of the world we inhabit
be transformed by the experience of letting go.
Guide my way of life
so that it is in tune with your New Creation.
Help me to loosen whatever bonds
prevent me from following you.

Glory to you, Source of All Being,
Eternal Word and Holy Spirit,
as it was in the beginning,
is now and will be forever.
Amen.

Notes

1 *Selected Writings*, p. 330.
2 Mark 10:17-22.
3 Maria Lopez Vigil, from a story by Coralia Godoy in *Piezas Para Un Retrato*, trans. Eugene Palumbo (San Salvador: Universidad Centroamericana Jose Simeon Canas, 1993), pp. 139-140.
4 *Selected Writings*, p. 107.
5 *Piezas Para Un Retrato*.
6 *Selected Writings*, pp. 108-109.
7 Jim Forest, *Love Is the Measure*, p. 106.
8 *Selected Writings*, pp. 229-230.
9 Psalm 139:23-24.

DAY THREE
Pastors and Prophets

Coming Together in the Spirit

He had no property of his own..., but the cathedral
was especially dear to him. He saw in it a symbol of
the church and of the nation, with all their nobility
and in all their tragedy. He made the cathedral his
workplace 'par excellence,' the place where the
people met, the place that linked hundreds of priests
and nuns, the place from which his message went
out to the nation, and to the nations of the world. But
the cathedral has also been the place where persons
have been massacred, the place where they sought
sanctuary. It has been a hospital for the wounded, a
mortuary for the dead of the church and of the
people. Several times the cathedral has been seized
by popular organizations, several times closed and
opened. It has been a place for the liturgy—and for
hunger strikes.

This cathedral, a symbol of sorrow and of hope, a
meeting place for the church and for the people,
Romero made his own. Before the bodies of the dead
he bolstered the hopes of the people. He wanted the
cathedral to be what it ought above all to be: a chair
from which was proclaimed the good news, the
gospel. By nature he was rather shy. But in the
cathedral he was transfigured. In it he became aware
that the gospel was directed to all Salvadorans, to the

whole of the country. He made the cathedral the center both of the church and of the nation.[1]

Without doubt, it was a place to be prophet and pastor.

Defining Our Thematic Context

Both Dorothy and Oscar seemed to integrate the personal and the political instinctively, to be both pastor and prophet. Their deep roots in real life and faithful accompaniment of people in struggle gave them insight into the experience of human suffering and simultaneously into the social or political causes of that suffering. They knew that the journey of a soul before God was not divorced from the rutted journey through an imperfect and too often unjust, mean world.

Their lives were very different. Even the margins they touched and the brokenness they witnessed came from two different worlds, but each managed to find balance where few others have been able to do so.

Dorothy always had a prophetic streak. She immediately saw the political angle in a situation or an event. Even at a distance from the poor, she understood that social and economic forces in the United States and the world were not functioning to the benefit of the people she loved. Her early writings reveal a capacity for sharp, critical social analysis. When she moved in with the poor—or rather, when they moved in with her—she also became a pastor, ministering to their more immediate needs of body and soul.

Oscar was trained as a pastor and, by all accounts, he was a very good one. But the people he served soon taught him to see the political as well. He was led by them to be prophet—and prophet he was.

Opening Prayer

Jesus, brother, friend,
you were pastor and prophet.
You loved deeply
and nourished freely.
The hungry ones ignored by others
flocked to your care.
For all of us you were prophet, as well,
one who spoke the truth,
the one who was Truth.
Be with us as we consider
the witness of Dorothy and Oscar,
prophets and pastors of our own age. Amen.

Scripture

When he came to Nazareth, where he had been
brought up, he went to the synagogue on the sabbath
day, as was his custom. He stood up to read, and the
scroll of the prophet Isaiah was given to him. He
unrolled the scroll and found the place where it was
written:

"The Spirit of the Lord is upon me,
    because he has anointed me
        to bring good news to the poor.
He has sent me to proclaim release to the captives
    and recovery of sight to the blind,
        to let the oppressed go free,
to proclaim the year of the Lord's favor."

And he rolled up the scroll, gave it back to the
attendant, and sat down. The eyes of all in the
synagogue were fixed on him. Then he began to say
to them, "Today this scripture has been fulfilled in
your hearing." All spoke well of him and were

amazed at the gracious words that came from his mouth. They said, "Is not this Joseph's son?" He said to them, "Doubtless you will quote to me this proverb, 'Doctor, cure yourself!' And you will say, 'Do here also in your hometown the things that we have heard you did at Capernaum.'" And he said, "Truly I tell you, no prophet is accepted in the prophet's hometown."[2]

Retreat Session Three

After a long pause Oscar speaks first. He seems very tired, frustrated.

Oscar: How I love these people! How I feel their pain and how I yearn to speak clearly in the public arena on their behalf! Would that I had the power to heal them, to take onto my own shoulders the suffering they endure— suffering of body and soul. How often I visited their homes and communities and saw what they endure!

And they loved it when I came. Hear what one of them said:

> The community of San Roque was far away and no one could get there in a car. It was on a path—not an ordinary path. It was in a ravine where even now buses cannot go.
>
> Nevertheless, Monseñor Romero was going to visit there. When the news was confirmed it was unbelievable, but it was true. He came to celebrate First Communions.
>
> He got out of his car on the road and walked and walked, walked and walked. Everyone he greeted

along the way joined him so that he was surrounded by a ring of people as if it were a procession. People were not crying about troubles, but singing about their joy.

On this walk to the village I met him and also joined the procession going up and down ravines. There I spoke with him for the first time....

Some people called to him from inside their little houses. "Monseñor, come in!" And he never avoided anyone, never refused the invitation. He stayed for a little while in each house to greet the family....[3]

Dorothy: I understand well your weariness, my friend. Day after day they flock to the doors of our houses of hospitality. So many of them—each one in need of healing. How often we thought we had reached the limits of our resources! Yet the hunger for healing evokes the best from the weakest among us. We learn to listen a bit more carefully, to touch a little more tenderly, to give more generously, to see time we give to pastoring as time given to God.

Oscar: But love cannot stop there.

Dorothy: No, or the suffering will never end.

Oscar: The Spirit requires that we speak out, but sometimes the burden of public witness is nearly unbearable. I think a lot about Jesus in the Temple—how he was rejected and threatened even as he spoke about the Good News. I guess the Good News about a world of justice for all doesn't sound very good at first to those who are doing well by the status quo.

Dorothy: But the responsibility to speak out about

injustice and oppression when we are tending to their bitter fruits, healing the wounds they make, is pretty clear.

Oscar: At first when I saw my flock attacked by wolves, I thought the wolves didn't mean to harm them. I thought I could convert the few who had gone mad. But then I began to see the breadth and depth of the evil. I began to understand the meaning of social sin. And I could not be silent. I remember trying to explain:

> Let no one take ill that in the light of God's words...we enlighten social, political, and economic realities. If we did not, it would not be Christianity for us. It is thus that Christ willed to become incarnate, so that the light he brings...may become the life of men [and women] and nations.... I know that many are scandalized by this word and want to accuse it of forsaking the preaching of the gospel to meddle in politics. I do not accept that accusation.... I ask the Lord during the week, while I receive the cries of the people and the sorrow of so much crime, the disgrace of such violence, to give me the fitting word to console, to denounce, to call to repentance.[4]

Dorothy: How often I have offended people, even my friends, when the Good News seemed to go too far. Perhaps hardest for all of us was our call to pacifism during World War II. We had clearly condemned anti-Semitism in all its ugliness, but we could not abide by war as the answer. We maintained our pacifist witness in spite of its tremendous unpopularity. At the time, I wrote to our communities around the country:

> We are at war, a declared war, with Japan, Germany and Italy. But still we can repeat Christ's words, each day, holding them close in our hearts, each month printing them in the paper.... Let us remember St.

Francis who spoke of peace, and we will remind our readers of him, too, so they will not forget.... We are still pacifists. Our manifesto is the Sermon on the Mount, which means that we will try to be peacemakers. Speaking for many of our conscientious objectors, we will not participate in armed warfare or in making munitions, or by buying government bonds to prosecute the war, or in urging others to these efforts. But neither will we be carping in our criticism. We love our country and we love our President.... We will try daily, hourly, to pray for an end to the war.... [U]nless we continue this prayer with almsgiving, in giving to the least of God's children; and fasting in order that we may help feed the hungry; and penance in recognition of our share in the guilt, our prayer may become empty words.

Our Works of Mercy may take us into the midst of war. As editor of *The Catholic Worker* I would urge our friends and associates to care for the sick and wounded, to the growing of food for the hungry, to the continuance of all our Works of Mercy in our houses and on our farms. We understand, of course, that there is and that there will be great differences of opinion even among our own groups as to how much collaboration we can have with the government in times like these. There are differences more profound and there will be many continuing to work with us from necessity, or from choice, who do not agree with us as to our position on war, and conscientious objection, etc. But we beg that there will be mutual charity and forbearance among us all.[5]

For Reflection

Followers of Christ in our own times are also called by the

*Spirit to bring the Good News to the poor as well as to proclaim
the year of jubilee. Preaching the Good News is both a pastoral
and a prophetic task.*

- *In what concrete ways are you pastor in your own family,
  neighborhood, school, parish? Do you take the time to listen
  well and tend to the brokenness around you? Do you
  respond to immediate needs within your reach? How?*

- *Do you ever shelter the homeless or feed the hungry,
  literally? Or clothe the naked or visit the sick or imprisoned
  or comfort the bereaved? If not, why not?*

*The words which follow come from Kairos USA, an interfaith
association of racially and ethnically diverse faith-based groups
whose mission is to reflect on the signs of the times and discern
a faith-filled response to social issues. These words may help us
reflect on the prophetic dimension of our own discipleship
journeys. Similar documents have been written by groups in
South Africa, Central America and in other parts of the global
south, who, "in the midst of crisis, sought to name a kairos, a
decisive time inviting creative and costly response from
communities of faith." The Kairos USA document suggests the
contemporary prophetic challenge quite well.*

> Our greatest challenge is simply to act humanly in
> the midst of violence and death, to exercise sanity
> and conscience, to practice resurrection...to join the
> thriving new theological convergence which crosses
> traditional church barriers, to change the landscape
> and the soulscape of our communities.
>
> We are led by the Spirit to form alliances across
> difference, embracing diverse gifts and the gifts of
> diversity—to ally ourselves with people of other
> faiths and with those who claim no faith at all—to
> build a multiracial, multicultural movement for
> justice and peace.
>
> We are led by the Spirit to a new relationship with

the earth and all its creatures based on a deep sense of kinship—to reject the obsessive patterns of consumption which drive the disintegration of creation.

We are led by the Spirit to shape a culture of radical nonviolence, a living alternative to the reality of our times, consciously countering racism, sexism, heterosexism, domestic violence, street violence, state violence, militarism.

We are led by the Spirit to rebuild the fabric of our families and our communities; to affirm and foster covenantal relationships with sexual integrity; and to further a culture of personal responsibility and social reconstruction.

We are led by the Spirit to birth new forms of community: reflective and analytical, contextual and prophetic, contemplative and active, diverse and creative.

We are led by the Spirit to create new visions and possibilities through art, music, poetry, story telling, a renewal of language itself—nurturing both memory and imagination as spiritual disciplines.

We are led by the Spirit to relinquish and renounce economic privilege that allows us as persons and families, as communities and churches, to ignore the social mortgage on property, both real and financial—to join the continuing struggles for Native land rights, for family farms, and for accessible, ecologically sound common land in urban areas.

We are led by the Spirit to free economic imagination, to promote alternative economic practice and economic relationships in our institutions and communities that ensure the needs of all not the desires of a few; that value equally the work of each one; that honor the dignity of all and promote the rights of every one to a fully human existence.

We are led by the Spirit to restructure radically the global economy to benefit the excluded poor and to protect the rest of creation—to lift the burden of debt from the backs of the world's poor.[6]

Read the challenge of the Kairos document carefully again.

- *In what ways do you support the prophetic task of the Christian community?*

- *How do you give meaning to Jubilee justice in your own life? How can you learn to denounce injustice with clarity and courage and promote patterns of socio-economic and political life that are more consistent with the gospel?*

- *Do you sing out the Good News in celebration? How?*

Closing Prayer

Search me, O God, and know my heart;
 test me and know my thoughts.
See if there is any wicked way in me,
 and lead me in the way everlasting.[7]

O God, grant me the patience
to minister to our broken world.
Give me the courage to speak out
against injustice and for the Jubilee.
Help us to enact the Jubilee concretely
in our communities, our institutions, our lives.

Glory to you, Source of All Being,
Eternal Word and Holy Spirit,
as it was in the beginning,
is now and will be forever.
Amen.

Notes

1 From "A Theologian's View of Oscar Romero," by Jon Sobrino, S.J., in *Archbishop Oscar Romero: Voice of the Voiceless, The Four Pastoral Letters and Other Statements,* trans. Michael J. Walsh (Maryknoll, N.Y.: Orbis Books, 1985), p. 34.

2 Luke 4:16-24.

3 From a story by Hilda Orantes in *Piezas Para Un Retrato,* pp. 254-255.

4 *The Word Remains,* p. 216.

5 *Selected Writings,* p. 262.

6 *On the Way: Kairos to Jubilee,* Kairos USA, 5757 N. Sheridan Road, #16A, Chicago, IL 60660.

7 Psalm 139:23-24.

DAY FOUR
The Joy of Community

Coming Together in the Spirit

We were just sitting there talking when Peter Maurin came in.

We were just sitting there talking when lines of people began to form, saying, "We need bread." We could not say, "Go, be thou filled." If there were six small loaves and a few fish, we had to divide them. There was always bread.

We were just sitting there talking and people moved in on us. Let those who can take it, take it. Some moved out and made room for more. And somehow the walls expanded.

We were just sitting there talking and someone said, "Let's all go live on a farm." It was as casual as all that, I often think. It just came about. It just happened.

I found myself, a barren woman, the joyful mother of children. It is not easy always to be joyful, to keep in mind the duty of delight.

The most significant thing about the Catholic Worker is poverty, some say.

The most significant thing is community, others say. We are not alone anymore.

But the final word is love. At times it has been, in the words of Father Zossima, a harsh and dreadful thing, and our faith in love has been tried through fire.

We cannot love God unless we love each other.
We know Him in the breaking of bread, and we
know each other in the breaking of bread, and we are
not alone anymore. Heaven is a banquet and life is a
banquet, too, even with a crust, where there is
companionship.

We have all known the long loneliness and we
have learned that the only solution is love and love
comes with community.

It all happened while we sat there talking, and it
is still going on.[1]

Defining Our Thematic Context

In the previous session we heard Archbishop
Romero's struggle to find space for the Church to proclaim
the gospel of life through its pastoral as well as its
prophetic ministry. Dorothy helped us understand the
profound and real challenge of gospel ministry in her own
world.

Dorothy and Oscar would have defined community in
very different ways as well. Dorothy's experience of
community was ultimately central to her identity. From
the moment she, at Peter Maurin's urging, opened the
door to homeless and hungry people, community was a
part of Dorothy's life. Hers was a particular kind of radical
community, a house of hospitality that welcomed all who
came and treated them with love and dignity.

Community was also an important part of Oscar's life,
but in a very different way. He saw Christian communities
flower in El Salvador and knew them as a source of
challenge—of life and strength. Though he had close
friends—families he loved to be with—and he was
welcomed by the Sisters of Divine Providence to a guest

space at their hospital, Oscar ultimately lived alone. Yet, as he opened himself to the Christian communities of his own land and shed his fear of the consequences of their faithful and courageous actions for justice, Oscar became a beloved member of every Salvadoran family and community.

Opening Prayer

You have blessed us, O God,
with companions for the journey,
communities that nourish and challenge us,
that help us hear your word
in new ways
and act on it.
Fill us with the joy of friendship.
Where two or three gather in your name,
be with us, we plead.
Amen.

Scripture

When they [Jesus' disciples] had prayed, the place in which they were gathered together was shaken; and they were all filled with the Holy Spirit and spoke the word of God with boldness.

Now the whole group of those who believed were of one heart and soul, and no one claimed private ownership of any possessions, but everything they owned was held in common. With great power the apostles gave their testimony to the resurrection of the Lord Jesus, and great grace was upon them all. There was not a needy person among them, for as many as owned lands or houses sold them and brought the proceeds of what was sold. They laid it at the apostles' feet, and it was distributed to each as any had need.[2]

RETREAT SESSION FOUR

Dorothy smiles as she gently changes the subject.

Dorothy: The journey is long and lonely. As followers of Jesus we so often find ourselves in a strange place—beyond the understanding of society, even of family and friends. But, oh what a gift we can find in community!

Oscar: Yes, the loneliness. Sometimes it has weighed very heavily on my shoulders. Yet sometimes I *had* to be alone. Ultimately that is how we stand before God.

Dorothy: I was overwhelmed. They came from everywhere with new ideas and new energy. They took over my life, my space, my mind, my heart. They were the people of God. Together, we shaped community.

My attitude toward those who came to the Catholic Worker was often criticized. I wasn't helping the "deserving poor," it was said, but rather drunkards, loafers and thieves. Why were there no employment or rehabilitation programs? Didn't I realize that the clothes that the Worker gave away were often sold or bartered for drink? Anyway, didn't Jesus himself say that the poor would be with us always? "Yes," I replied again and again, "but we are not content that there should be so many of them. The class structure is of our making and by our consent, not God's, and we must do what we can to change it. We are urging revolutionary change."

A social worker asked me one day how long the down-and-out were permitted to stay at the Worker. "'We let them stay forever,' I answered. 'They live with us, they die with us and we give them a Christian burial. We pray for them after they are dead. Once they are taken in, they become members of the family. Or rather they always were members of the family. They are our brothers and sisters in Christ.'"[3]

Oscar: I was nervous at first about the phenomenon called "Christian base communities" in El Salvador. I knew they were struggling to improve their living conditions, to demand basic rights and a minimum of security—and rightfully so—but I was afraid they would forget about God!

Little did I know their faithfulness and the cost of discipleship they were willing to pay. When I let down the barriers, when I opened my soul to them, they embraced me with their strong arms.

Dorothy: Yes, community does embrace with strong arms. It also challenges. Many Catholic Worker communities have formed in the United States. Each one is faithful in its own way to the gospel of Jesus Christ. These communities, with all their flaws, have been a remarkable place of support for me. Along the way I have had many doubts about this "work of God" in my life. What an unlikely person I was to guide a radical movement in the Catholic Church of the 1930's, a Church that was very clear about the "appropriate" role of women and mothers. I was a single mother, working outside my home, and a convert to Catholicism with a long list of "suspicious" leftist connections!

Peter Maurin was the visionary who helped us all see

the value of common life. He challenged us to live in completely new ways that made it easy for people to be good, and we did. We really tried to live as if the New Creation were actually breaking into our world! As one of our admirers later wrote:

> [The] Worker community consisted of whoever showed up at the door. The result was often an assemblage of characters that seemed drawn from a novel by Dostoevsky. On hand in most Catholic Worker houses was a similar cast of pilgrims, scholars, and "holy fools," the young and old, workers, loafers, and everything in between. It was a microcosm of sorts, a family, as Dorothy would say, and an example of the possibility of a diverse group of individuals residing together in relative harmony, without the need of elaborate rules. The basis for community was not an ideal to be achieved, but the recognition of a reality already accomplished by Christ—the fact that all, whether clever or dull, fit or infirm, beautiful or plain, were "members one of another."[4]

Oscar: "Living as if" is a wonderful expression. That is exactly what Salvadoran communities were trying to do. Jesus came to announce the inbreaking of the New Creation in a sinful world. He called us to live and act like brothers and sisters and to work together to make that promise come true in the concrete situations of our daily lives. Our communities blossomed from that joint effort.

Dorothy: Yes, so did ours. I think the balance between the common task of tending to the real needs of the children of God comprising our communities and the need to attend to the needs of a violated and broken world is very delicate in communities. Somehow even in our communities we have to incorporate the pastoral and the prophetic. In a culture that celebrates individualism, community life is very hard.

Oscar: I can imagine. At least the shared physical needs of our poor communities, our shared faith and our celebration of extended families and neighborhood connections make the details of community life less troublesome for us. Our lives are less separated, I think. Here the challenge is in developing a spiritually reflective and socially critical attitude in our communities—even in building the self-esteem of our people to understand their own worth in the plan of God. They have been impoverished for so long!

Dorothy: People in my country are yearning for community, but don't know where to find one! Sometimes our families are communities; sometimes parishes or prayer groups are communities; sometimes neighborhoods are communities. But too often each one lives in isolation from others. We tend to emphasize individualism, thinking of community as a potential invasion of privacy, not a blessed interaction. That is especially true among more prosperous people in the United States. But we are a very hungry people—hungry for meaning in our lives—and for good relationships that nurture our souls.

Oscar: It would be so good if Salvadoran communities could accompany communities in your country as they form, adding another dimension to your own vision. We have found such life and wholeness as our communities have matured. I suspect that the values and qualities we have found helpful would make sense in your reality as well. For example, the bishops of Latin America have described a basic Christian community in the following way. It is an excellent description!

It brings together families, adults, and young people,
in an intimate interpersonal relationship grounded in
the faith. As an ecclesial reality, it is a community of
faith, hope, and charity. It celebrates the Word of
God and...it fleshes out the Word of God in life
through solidarity and commitment to the new
commandment of the Lord; and through the service
of approved coordinators, it makes present and
operative the mission of the Church and its visible
communion with the legitimate pastors. It is a base-
level community because it is composed of relatively
few members as a permanent body, like a cell of the
larger community.

To live in community is not a matter of choice but
of calling. Christianity demands, by its calling, the
formation of community. Christianity cannot be
thought of except in terms of relationships with other
persons, brothers and sisters in whom we make real
the comradely love that we preach. There is nothing
in revelation about the *de facto* forms that
communities should take.... It is the particular
moment in history, the particular place in which they
operate, that should give the precise shape to
communities, as the occasion demands.[5]

Dorothy: That is exactly what Peter preached! And they
have to be communities in real contact with the poorest
and most marginalized groups—in fact, the communities
themselves should include the poorest and most
marginalized people.

Oscar: It is very helpful if communities can be diverse in
age and class, gift and vocation. Most Salvadoran
Christian base communities are families coming
together—men, women, children of all ages. There is good

leadership in our best communities, but it is usually shared leadership so as to draw upon the talents and insights of the different members. Servant leadership is key.

Dorothy: In our country, racial and ethnic difference is a great blessing for any community. Most Catholic Worker communities are open to anyone who cares to walk with them for a while. In other good communities, there is a process of mutual discernment before a new person joins. Basic compatibility of values helps.

Oscar: Common values are key for community life. I think among the most important are courage and honesty, patience and fidelity to the gospel.

Dorothy: Christian communities do come in all shapes. People come together in community for a variety of reasons, but I think they have to nurture an inner life in the Spirit and an outer life attentive to the needs of the world. Both are part of the integrated whole. Life in the Spirit in order to encourage, support, love, enjoy and challenge each other, has to help each one heal the wounds of life. Life in the struggle for a better world that is peaceful and just needs the support of community. Yet community life, with all its blessings, is still very difficult, even trying. Sometimes the trivialities have made me cry. I remember mourning when my favorite tree in front of the Catholic Worker was broken off. I remember being upset by the mess or the chaos. I remember being frustrated by the idiosyncrasies of one or another community member. Hard times come in all kinds of communities, but if we are willing to risk in order to follow Jesus, I believe we can find great joy and deep satisfaction in communal life.

For Reflection

Assisi Community is a small intentional Catholic
Christian community of individuals and families—
women and men, teenagers, children, professed
religious and laypeople, North Americans and
Central Americans—who are striving to live
faithfully the gospel call to work for a more just and
peaceful world, who are trying to put into practice
the values of Jesus—"living our way," so to speak,
into the New Creation. We welcome those from other
faith traditions as well who would like to share our
journey.

Ours is a community focused outward toward the
world in which we live. Each member's work for
social transformation nourishes our communal life
and we offer conscious support to each other in these
efforts. At times we participate as a community in a
particular project or witness for social justice. We are
sisters to a base community in El Salvador and a
sanctuary for refugees at risk, welcoming them as
equals into the community not as our gift but as their
right. We are working to overcome the sin of sexism,
to honor the masculine and the feminine as equally
valuable. We seek to accompany those who suffer
from poverty, injustice, oppression.

Our communal life-style is intentionally simple as
an expression of solidarity with those who live in
want, as a sign of life-giving values in a consumer
society and as a way of "using lightly" the gifts of
creation. Many in our community are moving their
lives toward voluntary poverty as well. An ongoing
exploration of this journey toward poverty continues
to offer rich material for reflection and discernment
among us.

For now we have chosen to express our desire for
simplicity through a very basic diet, frugal use of
appliances and utilities, simple household

furnishings, sharing of cars, etc. We eat meat very infrequently, never red meat, for reasons that include a consciousness of a hungry world; awareness of the emotional anguish of those who slaughter animals for food; and the fact that grain-fed beef is neither an efficient nor a healthful source of food.

We strive as well to nourish the inner needs of the community and community members. Our common life is centered on morning prayers, an evening meal and weekly "house meetings." Each adult's commitment to participate in these activities whenever possible is taken seriously, as is participation in more substantive reflections about once a month, retreats twice a year and special celebrations on important feasts.

Assisi Community is richly blessed with the diverse gifts of each one's experience. We are particularly touched by the tradition of Francis and Clare, by the base communities of Latin America and by the charisms of religious communities whose members have joined us. We are striving to articulate a new spirituality informed by the joining of lay spirituality with that of religious.

There is no single authority figure in the community. Different community members with particular experience or knowledge play leadership roles in different situations. The tasks of homemaking (cooking, cleaning, shopping, etc.) are equally shared.

We intentionally emphasize mutuality and participation and find that real dialogue about important community issues (as well as global issues) is a vital part of life. We make a conscious effort to be sensitive and enabling of each other. Decisions are made by consensus.

Beyond this we are aware that our community has been and will continue to be shaped by the Christian tradition of community, of which we know we are a part. We are also aware that ours is a new community—that our mission, our self-description, our dreams will be shaped and transformed by the reality of the life we share and the signs of the times in which we live.[6]

Above is part of the mission statement of one contemporary community in the United States. If you are a member of a community that has articulated its own vision, use it for reflection instead of this. Look for the values and commitments carried in the statement. Draw from the above mission statement and from Acts 4:32-35 and expand upon them in prayer. Think about your own idea of an ideal community.

- *What contribution could you make to community life?*

- *What could you give to the world through a community?*

- *What would you need from a community?*

- *Where do you encounter community in your own life?*

- *What are the obstacles to community in you? Around you?*

Closing Prayer

Search me, O God, and know my heart;
  test me and know my thoughts.
See if there is any wicked way in me,
  and lead me in the way everlasting.[7]

You are Community, dear God.
You have called us to community.
Help us to recognize the communities in our lives.
Help us to build communities in our world.

Glory to you, Source of All Being,
Eternal Word and Holy Spirit,

as it was in the beginning,
is now and will be forever.
Amen.

Notes

[1] *Selected Writings*, pp. 362, 363.

[2] Acts 4:31-35.

[3] *Love Is the Measure*, p. 67.

[4] *Selected Writings*, p. xxix.

[5] *Voice of the Voiceless*, pp. 153-154.

[6] Mission Statement, Assisi Community, Washington, D.C.

[7] Psalm 139:23-24.

DAY FIVE
The Radical Gospel

Coming Together in the Spirit

Listen now to an eyewitness account of an attack by
Salvadoran helicopters on families fleeing from El
Salvador across the Lempa River into Honduras on March
18, 1980. Yvonne Dilling, who narrates this account, and
two other relief workers had been alerted that seven
thousand refugees were trying to escape from the daily
aerial bombardment.

We had barely arrived at that rocky shore full of
crying babies and half-naked adults when behind me
came two priests who had been working in this
diocese. We all three smiled at one another and
headed into the river. The current was strong and the
river deep.... Someone had tied a heavy rope across
and all were using that against the current. I've no
idea how many children I carried across on my back.
Some were so small we tied them onto me. Others
were old enough to hold on, yet most of them were
terrified, crying, gripping like steel.... We had been
swimming about an hour when the helicopter
arrived.... Everyone ran for shelter under the gigantic
rocks which are strewn on the bank. I was helping
push children out of sight with one of the young
seminary students. There was no space left so for the
next fifteen minutes we ran around a very large

rock—running from sight of the helicopter as it machine-gunned and bombed the river, turned around and repeated from the other direction.... No one was killed in those fifteen minutes. My feet and legs were bruised from running on and over the rocks. Then the copter left. Without thought I went right back into the river to the other side. I made maybe five trips—one with a child too large for me; we really struggled to make it. I was resting and catching my breath when the helicopter returned.

We ran farther up the shore under a large full-branched tree. There must have been thirty of us huddled there—so vulnerable to the helicopter. Two small crying children climbed on me. Padre was beside me and we held hands and soothed babies for twenty minutes while the helicopter tried systematically to massacre us all.... We saw one little boy fall into the river, hit in the back.... Some panicked and ran. As soon as they ran, the helicopter would spot them and turn around for another round. I felt like we were live bait, especially when the children ran from one rock to another.

It seemed like we spent three hours under that tree. When the helicopter finally left, I felt numb.[1]

Archbishop Romero spoke very clearly about the role of the Church in the face of this kind of brutality. He said, "In this situation of conflict the Church has placed itself at the side of the poor and has undertaken...their defense."[2]

Defining Our Thematic Context

The lives of Oscar and Dorothy were changed by an encounter with the poor, the marginalized. They were very clear about the nourishment they drew from walking with those who were deliberately excluded from enjoying the benefits of society. They knew the important role community played in their lives. They knew that they were called to be both pastors and prophets—perhaps not in so many words—but they knew where they were called to be and they were faithful to that call.

In a world of competing ideologies, however, prophecy can quickly be twisted into partisan politics, just as silence can support the status quo. Archbishop Romero was forced to walk a particularly fine line. He could not be silent, yet the space for critical witness in El Salvador in the 1970's and 1980's was almost nonexistent. For Romero and the Church to stand by the people in opposition to the power of the oligarchy and the military was nearly the same as for Romero and the Church to join the revolution. But the Archbishop did not do so.

Dorothy Day's challenge was different, yet similar. The narrow path she walked upon was a political one between right and left. It was also critically nonpartisan and passionately committed to justice. As a personalist formed by Peter Maurin, she insisted on *personal* responsibility. As a radical painfully aware of the public roots of human suffering, she insisted on *social* responsibility. As a Christian, she witnessed to *communal* responsibility.

The gospel moves us beyond the ideology of left or right to a place of truth from which honest judgment and faithful commitment to justice can better be determined.

Opening Prayer

> Source of Life,
> Sun of Justice,
> you give us a narrow path
> to walk upon.

Yet, we cannot not choose sides.
Guide our decisions and our commitments;
lead us in our own times to follow you.
Help us to see
the traps of left and right,
yet to act
in harmony with your plan
for this world in which we dwell.

Scripture

Now when they saw the boldness of Peter and John
and realized that they were uneducated and ordinary
men, they were amazed and recognized them as
companions of Jesus. When they saw the man who
had been cured standing beside them, they had
nothing to say in opposition. So they ordered them
to leave the council while they discussed the matter
with one another. They said, "What will we do with
them? For it is obvious to all who live in Jerusalem
that a notable sign has been done through them; we
cannot deny it. But to keep it from spreading further
among the people, let us warn them to speak no
more to anyone in this name." So they called them
and ordered them not to speak or teach at all in the
name of Jesus. But Peter and John answered them,
"Whether it is right in God's sight to listen to you
rather than to God, you must judge; for we cannot
keep from speaking about what we have seen and
heard."[3]

RETREAT SESSION FIVE

Oscar: The road is very narrow, and sometimes we are misunderstood.

Dorothy: Say more. I'm not sure I know what you mean.

Oscar: Here in El Salvador our society is extremely polarized. On the one side are the wealthy few and the military who support them. Some of them—many of them—are my friends. Many are good, even generous people. Others are vicious, filled with evil and hate. Many are blind, refusing to see the consequences of the privileges they have come to expect.

Dorothy: I see.

Oscar: Perhaps. I think that the reality we live would be very hard for those who live in the United States to understand. On the other side are an oppressed and frustrated people who watch their children die from hunger while most of the land grows crops to make the rich richer. The injustice here is very clear. Years of hoping against hope, of patient waiting, have not changed anything.

Dorothy: I believe that the gospel calls us to oppose violence, to seek justice nonviolently.

Oscar: I believe that, too, but I also believe that institutionalized violence has to be overcome. I have tried to be a peacemaker. Even as violence closed in on us, I have tried to prevent the growth of a mysticism of violence, to promote justice, dialogue, truth and

73

magnanimity. I cannot in our tragic Salvadoran situation simply condemn all forms of violence in the same way. The repression is a profoundly provocative violence. It cannot in any way be justified or supported. Defensive or responsive violence is different, though in the end we have to find ways to overcome hate bred by violence, to withstand the temptation to vengeance.

The choices are so difficult. The teachings of our Church are clear that all human beings have a right to satisfy their basic needs. The popular movements in my country have organized and educated themselves and their communities to insist upon a radical transformation of our society, and the Church supports their right to make these demands. The journey is long and difficult. The pain along the way is intense. At the same time, the Church has uttered an "anguished cry of denunciation and repudiation. 'No to violence' it has cried out impartially against any hand raised against someone else, carrying out an act of violence that stains the world with sin."[4]

Dorothy: I, too, have seen and celebrated popular organization especially labor unions in the early years. As time went on, however, I began to feel that many of the major unions in the United States had no vision, no real commitment to the New Creation. For a long time we could not support their struggles. Selfish interests seemed to have clouded their sight. In spite of our own Catholic Worker connections; in spite of the Church's longtime support for labor and the right to organize, we had to back away.

Yet, we have walked a very long way with Cesar Chavez and the United Farm Workers of America. I believe that they are truly concerned with building community and promoting dignity and justice for some of the most oppressed people in our country. They are also, with the civil rights movement of an earlier decade, a powerful witness to the possibilities of active nonviolence. My prayer for them was very real and I addressed it to Pope John XXIII because I thought he would understand their struggle.

> Dear Pope John—please, yourself a *campesino*, watch over the United Farm Workers. Raise up more and more leader-servants throughout the country to stand with Cesar Chavez in this nonviolent struggle with Mammon, in all the rural districts of North and South, in the cotton fields, beet fields, potato fields, in our orchards and vineyards, our orange groves—wherever men, women, and children work on the land. Help make a new order wherein justice flourishes, and, as Peter Maurin, himself a peasant, said so simply, "where it is easier to be good."[5]

Oscar: The resistance to change is fierce here.

Dorothy: That is true in the United States as well, but it's more subtle. The United Farm Workers won enough to call off their long grape boycott, but migrant farmworkers in our country are devastatingly poor and continually oppressed.

Oscar: It seems to me that the Church has a special role. We are called to choose the side of justice and in that sense to choose sides. But the powerful ones who perpetrate injustice are also the children of God, beloved, invited to wholeness. We are called to give witness to the Reign of God, to work for a conversion of the structures and institutions of our societies—a conversion of our cultures that perpetuate violence and a conversion of hearts hardened by greed and selfishness and hate.

For Reflection

We live in a world that is racked with violence. We know it well. We feel it. Violence surrounds and enters our being: drug-related shootings in our neighborhoods, carjackings and muggings, wars and threats of war, horrific ethnic violence in Rwanda and Burundi, Bosnia-Herzogovina, East Timor, Bougainville, the Sudan, Guatemala, Nigeria, Mexico, Nicaragua. Violence is institutional and structural. It is poverty, hunger, environmental destruction, racism, sexism, the death penalty, abortion. It is the manufacture of handguns and of weapons of mass destruction, the sale and use of land mines. It is street violence, domestic violence, drug abuse. All around us violence begets violence; violence destroys life. And the poor—those on the margins—always pay the greatest price.

Read again Acts 4:13-20.

- *What is the message of the radical gospel in these violent times?*

- *What is the role of the people of God, the Church?*

- *How can we be engaged, deliberate, willing to take risks, to be foolish in order to help our broken world find a better way?*

- *Think of one person you know who is faithful to the gospel in a radical way. Why do you think that about her/him? Sometimes that witness is very threatening (think of John and Peter). Why? Name one value or characteristic of that person's life that you would like to imitate.*

Closing Prayer

Search me, O God, and know my heart;
test me and know my thoughts.
See if there is any wicked way in me,
and lead me in the way everlasting.[6]

You don't make this journey easy,
you who have called us to follow.
Encourage us,
accompany us.
Your word is difficult
and we are afraid.

Glory to you, Source of All Being,
Eternal Word and Holy Spirit,
as it was in the beginning,
is now and will be forever.
Amen.

Notes

[1] *Piezas Para Un Retrato.*
[2] *Voice of the Voiceless*, p. 181.
[3] Acts 4:13-20.
[4] *Voice of the Voiceless*, p. 166.
[5] *Selected Writings*, p. 257.
[6] Psalm 139:23-24.

DAY SIX
The Cost of Discipleship

Coming Together in the Spirit

Listen once again to an eyewitness account, this one by Tom Quigley, policy adviser for Latin America at the United States Catholic Conference, the bishops of the United States.

> Five of us from the U.S. churches had gone on a hastily formed ecumenical visit to El Salvador, seeking to express the solidarity of the U.S. religious community with him [Archbishop Romero] and the people of his country and to learn what we could of the current, rapidly changing situation. We were seated, Quaker, Episcopalian, Methodist and Catholic, in the sanctuary of the old ramshackle tin-roofed wooden Basilica of the Sacred Heart. The huge, cavernous poured-concrete cathedral ten blocks down the street, left unfinished by the previous archbishop who said, "We must stop building cathedrals and start building the Church," was unavailable.... The basilica [Sacred Heart] was packed, mostly with simple working people, families, kids on their fathers' shoulders. The entrance hymn began and with it, applause starting at the rear and undulating up to the front as the archbishop and the priests and seminarians, vested in brilliantly colored stoles over their albs, moved

joyfully up the aisle.

How describe a triumphal procession when there wasn't a trace of triumphalism anywhere? The applause was thunderous, shaking the corrugated roof, teasing tears out of the most unliturgical of our company; it was simply a pastor receiving the loving embrace of a people..., their suffering and their hopes, embodied in this humble figure.

It didn't occur to me then but it has since, that day, the eve of his martyrdom, was as vivid a re-creation as I could imagine of the palm-strewn path into Jerusalem.[1]

Archbishop Romero's homily on that occasion is now known and treasured throughout the world. In part he said:

I would like to make an appeal in a special way to the men of the army, and in particular to the ranks of the Guardia Nacional, of the police, to those in the barracks. Brothers, you are part of our own people. You kill your own *campesino* brothers and sisters. And before an order to kill that a man may give, the law of God must prevail that says: Thou shalt not kill! No soldier is obliged to obey an order against the law of God. No one has to fulfill an immoral law. It is time to recover your consciences and to obey your consciences rather than the orders of sin. The church, defender of the rights of God, of the law of God, of human dignity, the dignity of the person, cannot remain silent before such abomination. We want the government to take seriously that reforms are worth nothing when they come about stained with so much blood. In the name of God, in the name of this suffering people whose laments rise to heaven each day more tumultuous, I beg you, I ask you, I order you in the name of God: Stop the repression![2]

Defining Our Thematic Context

The reality of their lives, the fruit of their pastoring and their deep passion for social transformation ultimately brought Oscar and Dorothy (like most prophets) face to face with those in power. Each spoke truth with remarkable integrity and their message was clearly heard. Each chose time and again the route of active—very active—nonviolence.

The powerful turned on Oscar with a vengeance. They could not allow his message to touch their hearts of stone. Most Church hierarchy, the Salvadoran state, the oligarchy—one-time friends—and the military, all regarded him as an enemy. The consequences were predictable, but he did not change his course.

Dorothy's reality was different from Oscar's, yet she lived it with great courage day by day. Hers was the "little way," but powerful it was nonetheless! Not once did she shy away from engaging the powers and principalities in her world. She challenged the Church she loved as well as those with military might. She marched and fasted, supported miners and textile workers, farmworkers and gravediggers. She broke the law in the name of peace and justice and served time in jail.

Neither Oscar nor Dorothy provoked public critique lightly or randomly. Every time they acted the message was very clear. Every time they spoke out they were prepared to take the consequences. One inevitable step at a time they moved forward. They joined prophetic words with strategic action on behalf of justice and peace. Time and time again they carefully focused their message on those in power.

In this practice of speaking truth to power Oscar and Dorothy were following the example of Jesus. Oscar knew well that the message he repeated time and time again—

an invitation to active love—could lead him to the cross. But he could not turn back. Nor could Dorothy. Hers was a long tiring journey that more closely resembles our own. Or does it?

Opening Prayer

Loving God, Spirit of Life,
we pray for the courage
to speak truth to power.
We pray for wisdom to know how.
We pray for discernment.
Help us to denounce sin,
but love the sinner.
Help us to announce by our lives and actions
the power of your promise of life.
Amen.

Scripture

Jesus answered them, "The hour has come for the Son of Man to be glorified. Very truly, I tell you, unless a grain of wheat falls into the earth and dies, it remains just a single grain; but if it dies, it bears much fruit. Those who love their life lose it, and those who hate their life in this world will keep it for eternal life. Whoever serves me must follow me, and where I am, there will my servant be also."[3]

Oscar: They say that I am playing with fire. That is not what I intend at all.

Dorothy: I can see that. And you should not be silent. None of us can be silent in the face of injustice—not if we are serious about living the gospel. I remember so many times when I stirred calm waters into a tempest. I was arrested for the first time in Washington, D.C., when I broke the law to draw attention to the rights of women, especially to vote, but I was arrested many times after that as well. Time in jail was never easy.

All through those weary first days in jail when I was in solitary confinement, the only thoughts that brought comfort to my soul were those lines in the Psalms that expressed the terror and misery of man suddenly stricken and abandoned. Solitude and hunger and weariness of spirit—these sharpened my perceptions so that I suffered not only my own sorrow but the sorrow of those about me. I was no longer myself, I was [hu]man. I was no longer a young girl, part of a radical movement seeking justice for those oppressed. I was the oppressed. I was that drug addict, screaming and tossing in her cell, beating her head against the wall. I was that shoplifter who for rebellion was sentenced to solitary. I was that woman who had killed her children, who had murdered her lover.

And...hell was all about me. The sorrows of the world encompassed me. I was like one gone down into the pit. Hope had forsaken me. I was that mother whose child had been raped and slain. I was the mother who had borne the monster who had done it. I was even that monster, feeling in my own heart every abomination.[4]

Oscar: I can feel the rage directed at me. How can I show them that I love them, too? How can I choose sides for justice and against injustice—but for the wealthy and powerful people as well as for the poor people? The new creation is promised to all of us. But we have to *choose* to follow. I receive open threats against my life, but I am at peace. I cannot avoid what I must do. Time and again I have preached about the sin that is enveloping El Salvador. Once recently I said:

> It is not a matter of sheer routine that I insist once again on the existence in our country on structures of sin. They are sin because they produce the fruits of sin: the deaths of Salvadorans—the swift death brought by repression or the long, drawn out, but no less real, death from structural oppression. That is why we have denounced what in our country has become the idolatry of wealth, of the absolute right, within the capitalist system, of private property, of political power in national security regimes, in the name of which personal security is itself institutionalized....
>
> No matter how tragic it may appear, the church through its entrance into the real socio-political world has learned how to recognize, and how to deepen its understanding of, the essence of sin. The fundamental essence of sin, in our world, is revealed in the death of Salvadorans.[5]

Thousands upon thousands of Salvadorans have already been slaughtered. It must stop!

Dorothy: The Church as an institution must speak out for peace and justice, too. Perhaps you were aware of our activities in Rome? When the Second Vatican Council was drawing to a close twenty women, myself included, fasted for ten days to encourage the leaders in our Church to oppose the proliferation of nuclear weapons.

> I did not suffer at all from the hunger or headache or nausea which usually accompany the first few days of a fast, but I had offered my fast in part for the victims of famine all over the world, and it seemed to me that I had very special pains. They were certainly of a kind I have never had before, and they seemed to pierce to the very marrow of my bones when I lay down at night. Perhaps it was the hammock-shaped bed. Perhaps it was the cover, which seemed to weigh a ton, so that I could scarcely turn. At any rate, my nights were penitential enough to make up for the quiet peace of the days. Strangely enough, when the fast was over, all pains left me and I have not had them since.... [T]hese pains which went with the fast seemed to reach into my very bones, and I could only feel that I had been given some little intimation of the hunger of the world.[6]

Oscar: Yes, I remember hearing about your presence at the Council, but I must confess that I did not understand what you were doing. In El Salvador the poor fast because they have no choice. I understand now the depth of your opposition to the arms race. Not only does it threaten creation itself, but it also wastes the resources needed to sustain life.

Dorothy: A Church that preaches about social justice also must be just itself. I love the Church; I am its faithful daughter, but I don't understand its wealth and privilege. So much land, for example, owned by the Church and by Catholic institutions, is unproductive in a hungry world and untaxed when poor people and those struggling to survive are being taxed.

Oscar: I have begged and pleaded with the people in power in my country to change, to stop the repression. But it continues and deepens. It is as though evil itself is thrashing about in El Salvador.

Dorothy: But the martyrs of El Salvador are saints. They have joined the cloud of witnesses; they have walked in the footsteps of Jesus. We have both known them. The poor people we have loved so dearly are saints. The outcasts and lepers of our times are saints. The ones who struggle for justice are saints. The ones who have been killed by racism are saints. Over a decade ago the Rev. Dr. Martin Luther King, Jr., was shot as he stood on the balcony of a motel in Memphis, Tennessee.

I was sitting in the kitchen of one of the women's apartments on Kenmare Street watching the television when the news flash came. I sat there stunned, wondering if he was suffering a superficial wound, as James Meredith did on his Mississippi walk to overcome fear, that famous march on which the cry "Black Power" was first shouted. Martin Luther King wrote about it in his last book, *Where Do We Go From Here?*—a book which all of us should read because it makes us understand what the words "Black Power" really mean. Dr. King was a man of deepest and most profound spiritual insights.

These were the thoughts which flashed through my mind as I waited, scarcely knowing that I was waiting, for further news. The dreaded words were spoken almost at once. "Martin Luther King is dead!" The next day was Good Friday, the day commemorated by the entire Christian world as the day when Jesus Christ, true God and true Man, shed His blood.

"Unless the grain of wheat falls into the ground and dies, it remains alone. But if it dies it produces much fruit." Martin Luther King died daily, as St. Paul said. He faced death daily and said a number of times that he knew he would be killed for the faith that was in him. The faith that men [and women] could live together as brothers [and sisters]. The faith in the Gospel teaching of nonviolence. The faith that man [sic] is capable of change, of growth, of growing in love.[7]

Oscar: Amen.

Dorothy: Alleluia!

Very shortly after this imagined conversation, Oscar Romero, Archbishop of San Salvador, was shot as he celebrated Mass in the chapel of the Divine Providence Hospital in San Salvador. The Gospel read at that Mass, a memorial for the mother of a friend, was John 12:23-26, "Unless a grain of wheat fall...." In his final homily, Archbishop Romero said:

> [O]ne must not love oneself so much as to avoid getting involved in the risks of life that history demands of us.... those who try to fend off the danger will lose their lives, while those who out of love for Christ give themselves to the service of others will live, like the grain of wheat that dies, but only apparently. If it did not die, it would remain alone. The harvest comes about only because it dies, allowing itself to be sacrificed in the earth and destroyed. Only by undoing itself does it produce the harvest.... This is the hope that inspires us Christians. We know that every effort to better society, especially when injustice and sin are so ingrained, is an effort that God blesses, that God wants, that God demands of us.... Let us all do what we can.[8]

For Reflection

The final words of Oscar Romero are more than sufficient for our reflection: "One must not love oneself so much as to avoid getting involved in the risks of life that history demands of us.... Let us all do what we can." What do they mean in our lives?

- *Pray for a while with this thought. What are the risks of life that history demands of you in this time, in this place?*

- *Read again John 12:23-26. "Those who love their life will lose it, and those who hate their life in this world will keep it for eternal life." This profoundly challenging assertion cuts to the quick of our contemporary value system and calls into question the systems and structures of power and privilege to which we have become accustomed. Oscar's refusal to allow death threats to intimidate him or prevent him from speaking truth or calling for radical change made him a tremendous threat to the people in power in El Salvador.*

- *How does this translate into your life? In what ways can you lose your life in order to live?*

Closing Prayer

Search me, O God, and know my heart;
    test me and know my thoughts.
See if there is any wicked way in me,
    and lead me in the way everlasting.[9]

You have not led us down an easy path, O God.
Give us the courage to go on.

Glory to you, Source of All Being,
Eternal Word and Holy Spirit,

as it was in the beginning,
is now and will be forever.
Amen.

Notes

1 "Remembering a Bishop," by Thomas Quigley, in *The Witness*, Vol. 63, September 1980, p. 10.

2 From Romero's homily on March 23, 1980, one day before he was killed, in *The Word Remains*, p. 217.

3 John 12:23-26a.

4 From "From Union Square to Rome," in *Meditations, Dorothy Day*, by Stanley Vishnewski (Ramsey, N.J.: Paulist Press, 1970), pp. 8-9.

5 *Voice of the Voiceless*, pp. 183-184.

6 *Selected Writings*, pp. 332-333.

7 Ibid., pp. 339-340.

8 *Voice of the Voiceless*, pp. 191-193.

9 Psalm 139:23-24.

DAY SEVEN
Calling Others Forth

Coming Together in the Spirit

I have frequently been threatened with death. I must say that, as a Christian, I do not believe in death, but in resurrection. If they kill me, I will rise again in the people of El Salvador. I am not boasting; I say it with the greatest humility.

As a pastor, I am bound by a divine command to give my life for those whom I love, and that includes all Salvadorans, even those who are going to kill me. If they manage to carry out their threats, I shall be offering my blood for the redemption and resurrection of El Salvador.

Martyrdom is a grace from God that I do not believe I have earned. But if God accepts the sacrifice of my life, then may my blood be the seed of liberty, and a sign of the hope that will soon become a reality.

May my death, if it is accepted by God, be the liberation of my people, and as a witness of hope in what is to come. You can tell them, if they succeed in killing me, that I pardon them, and I bless those who may carry out the killing.

But I wish that they could realize that they are wasting their time. A bishop will die, but the church of God—the people—will never die.[1]

Defining Our Thematic Context

The lives and witness of Dorothy Day and Oscar Romero were extraordinary after all. It would be easy to put them on a candlelit pedestal, or their pictures, icons, on the wall—heroine and hero, but inimitably distant! In this last session of our retreat with Dorothy and Oscar, we reflect upon their invitation to each of us—an invitation to follow them following Jesus. Each expected others to follow their lead. In fact, both Dorothy and Oscar seemed to have an acute awareness that their work and witness were but a part of the whole. As they saw with the eyes of the poor, so must we.

Opening Prayer

In these days, O God,
you have called us once again into the desert.
You have invited us once again
to follow your disciples,
Oscar and Dorothy,
following you.
But your way is very difficult
and not always clear to us.
For we are weaker disciples,
not as strong as these two.
Yet, we are open.
Spirit of the yet-living God,
lead on.

RETREAT SESSION SEVEN

After Oscar Romero was assassinated in 1980, the people of El Salvador suffered ongoing war and repression for well over a decade. Thousands had already given their lives for liberation. Before the bitter war wound down in 1992, over seventy thousand civilians had been killed, most brutally, and over one and one-half million people had been displaced or forced into refuge outside of El Salvador. Though most died uncelebrated by other than family or community, a few particularly horrific cases gained international attention—some immediately, others much later.

A few had tremendous impact: the assassination of four U.S. churchwomen—Maura Clarke, M.M., Jean Donovan, Ita Ford, M.M., and Dorothy Kazel, O.S.U.—and the massacres at the Rio Lempa and El Mozote, where hundreds and hundreds of civilians were brutally killed in the early 1980's; the ruthless murder of six Jesuit priests, Ignacio Ellacuria, Amando Lopez, Joaquin Lopez y Lopez, Ignacio Martin-Baro, Segundo Montes and Juan Ramon Moreno, and two women coworkers, Julia Elba Ramos and Celina Ramos, at the Jesuit University at the end of that decade.

Throughout the long years of horror, the communities of El Salvador consciously walked the Way of the Cross. They did so courageously and with amazing hope. Despite flaws and detours, the story of their struggle is remarkable. Oscar truly rose again in his people.

Out of their own agony, Oscar Romero and the people of El Salvador gave a specific invitation to people of goodwill around the world: "Walk with us, accompany us on this torturous road; lighten our heavy loads. Find ways to help us stop the repression, stop the violence." Many people did—by participating in delegations to El Salvador, by accompanying returning refugees and displaced people, by educating the world about what was happening there, by demanding an end to U.S. military aid that was perpetuating the war, by providing sanctuary in other lands for Salvadorans at risk.

What happened to people of the wealthy world who opened themselves to the gift of the Salvadoran people was an extraordinary conversion of heart. In return, they were given an experience of community and living discipleship. From the most broken and impoverished places in the Americas, Salvadoran communities taught the meaning of forgiveness and reconciliation, gave the gift of hope, and kept alive the witness of their beloved "Monseñor."

Dorothy's legacy was rich as well. Much of her energy and gift was given to the Catholic Worker communities that multiplied, struggled and continued to flourish, principally in the United States, but in other parts of the world as well. Throughout Dorothy's life—and ever since—Catholic Worker communities have continued to live in different ways her vision and that of Peter Maurin. Combining hospitality to homeless people, community life and resistance to the arms race and to all forms of injustice and oppression, Catholic Workers are leaven in and challenge to a society too often overcome with self-indulgence and apathy. Their view of the world is consistently from the margins, as was Dorothy's, enabling them to see and respond to persistent death-dealing cultural patterns. The Catholic Worker groups in New York and in other cities continue to publish newspapers. Discussions for "clarification of thought" offer to the public opportunity for honest debate and deliberation about critical social issues. Following Dorothy's example, many Catholic Workers have participated in public acts of resistance to the violence of our world; some have spent months or years in jail.

Our two contemporary saint-mentors, Dorothy and Oscar, now invite us to reflect on our retreat experience.

For Reflection

Take a little time to think again about the various themes for our retreat with Oscar and Dorothy: Conversion; Accompaniment; Pastors and Prophets; Community; the Radical Gospel; and the Cost of Discipleship. Look over your notes or journal entries. Think about any stories or ideas that were of particular interest. Dorothy and Oscar left us with a specific invitation—to see, to love, to care for a broken world both far away and near to home.

- *How has this journey with two saints of our own times helped shape your idea of discipleship?*

- *Read once again Luke 6:20-26. How specifically did Oscar and Dorothy earn that invitation that we are so certain they heard: "Come, you who are blessed..." (see Matthew 25:34)?*

- *List some of the key characteristics of their lives. Can you identify similar characteristics in your own life?*

- *Which additional characteristics of Dorothy's life or Oscar's do you feel called to imitate, to incorporate into your life?*

Closing Prayer

O Lord, you have searched me and known me.
You know when I sit down and when I rise up;
    you discern my thoughts from far away.
You search out my path and my lying down,

and are acquainted with all my ways.
Even before a word is on my tongue,
    O Lord, you know it completely.
You hem me in, behind and before,
    and lay your hand upon me.
Such knowledge is too wonderful for me;
    it is so high that I cannot attain it.

Where can I go from your spirit?
    Or where can I flee from your presence?
If I ascend to heaven, you are there;
    If I make my bed in Sheol, you are there.

If I take the wings of the morning
    and settle at the farthest limits of the sea,
even there your hand shall lead me,
    and your right hand shall hold me fast.
If I say, "Surely the darkness shall cover me,
    and the light around me become night,"
even the darkness is not dark to you;
    the night is as bright as the day,
    for darkness is as light to you.[2]

Holy One, Hound of Heaven,
I give you thanks
for the journey of this retreat.
Spirit of Life, Enduring Gift,
pour forth your wisdom.
Grant me understanding.
Gift me with knowledge
that I may know and follow you.

For it was you who formed my inward parts;
    you knit me together in my mother's womb.
I praise you, for I am fearfully and wonderfully made.
    Wonderful are your works....

How weighty to me are your thoughts, O God!
   How vast is the sum of them!
I try to count them—they are more than the sand;
   I come to the end—I am still with you....

Search me, O God, and know my heart;
   test me and know my thoughts.
See if there is any wicked way in me,
   and lead me in the way everlasting.[3]

Glory to you, Source of All Being,
Eternal Word and Holy Spirit,
as it was in the beginning,
is now and will be forever.
Amen.

Going Forth to Live the Theme

Out of their deep love for Scripture, our holy mentors
send us forth not with inspired words of their own
making, but with a timeless parable from their Teacher—
and ours.

When the Son of Man comes in his glory, and all the
angels with him, then he will sit on the throne of his
glory. All the nations will be gathered before him,
and he will separate people from one another as a
shepherd separates the sheep from the goats, and he
will put the sheep at his right hand and the goats at
the left. Then the king will say to those at his right
hand, "Come, you that are blessed by my Father,
inherit the kingdom prepared for you from the
foundation of the world; for I was hungry and you
gave me food, I was thirsty and you gave me
something to drink, I was a stranger and you
welcomed me. I was naked and you gave me
clothing, I was sick and you took care of me, I was in

prison and you visited me." Then the righteous will answer him, "Lord, when was it that we saw you hungry and gave you food, or thirsty and gave you something to drink? And when was it that we saw you a stranger and welcomed you, or naked and gave you clothing? And when was it that we saw you sick or in prison and visited you?" And the king will answer them, "Truly I tell you, just as you did it to one of the least of these who are members of my family, you did it to me."[4]

Motivated by our retreat experience, may we commit ourselves to these works of mercy and claim the reward of those who stand with Dorothy Day and Oscar Romero at the right hand of the Lord.

Notes

[1] *Voice of the Voiceless*, pp. 50-51.

[2] Psalm 139:1-12.

[3] Psalm 139:13, 17, 23-24.

[4] Matthew 25:31-45.

Deepening Your Acquaintance

With Archbishop Oscar Romero

Books

Brockman, James R., S.J. *The Word Remains: A Life of Oscar Romero*. Maryknoll, N.Y.: Orbis Books, 1985.

Lopez Vigil, Maria. *Piezas Para Un Retrato*. San Salvador: Universidad Centroamericana Jose Simeon Canas, 1993.

Romero, Oscar A. *Voice of the Voiceless: The Four Pastoral Letters and Other Statements*. Maryknoll, N.Y.: Orbis Books, 1985.

Videos

A Question of Conscience: The Murder of the Six Jesuit Priests in El Salvador. Icarus/Tamouz Media Production. Available from Palisades Home Video.

Romero. Vidmark Entertainment. Available from Videos With Values.

Roses in December. First Run Features. Available from Ave Maria Press.

With Dorothy Day

Books

Day, Dorothy. *Loaves and Fishes*. New York: Curtis Books, 1963.

_____. *The Long Loneliness: The Autobiography of Dorothy Day*. New York: Image Books, 1959 (originally published in 1952 by Harper and Row).

_____. *On Pilgrimage: The Sixties*. New York: Curtis Books, 1972.

Ellsberg, Robert, ed. *Dorothy Day, Selected Writings: By Little and By Little*. Maryknoll, N.Y.: Orbis Books, 1992 (originally published by Alfred A. Knopf in 1983 as *By Little and By Little: The Selected Writings of Dorothy Day*).

Forest, Jim. *Love Is the Measure: A Biography of Dorothy Day*. Maryknoll, N.Y.: Orbis Books, 1985.

Roberts, Nancy L. *Dorothy Day and the Catholic Worker*. Albany: State University of New York Press, 1984.

Videos

Dorothy Day: Blessed Are the Poor. Catholic Life in America Series. Available from Videos With Values.

Haunted by God (A Play About Dorothy Day). Fisher Productions. Available from Paulist Press.